UNDERSTANDING
SANCTIONS

The International Fr... ...UK)

WITHDRAWN FROM THE LIBRARY

D0654170

KING ALFRED'S COLLEGE
WINCHESTER

330.968
H01 | 28967

First published 1988
International Freedom Foundation (UK)
10 Storey's Gate
London SW1P 3AY
© International Freedom Foundation 1988
ISBN 1 871117 00 3

THE INTERNATIONAL FREEDOM FOUNDATION

WHY A FREEDOM FOUNDATION

The International Freedom Foundation is an organisation dedicated to the promotion of individual freedom throughout the world. The Foundation proposes to promote freedom in two ways: (a) by elucidating and highlighting the principles of free and unfettered individual association; and (b) by exposing the cynical use of the concept of freedom by totalitarian systems in order to enslave their citizens.

FOUNDING PRINCIPLES

Embodied in the Foundation's concept and promotion of freedom are the three founding principles of liberty, prosperity and security. Liberty, which allows the individual to find the greatest expression of his highest values in society, free from Government interference. Prosperity, which is embodied in the free enterprise system and contingent on the existence of liberty; and security which is the ultimate guarantor of the individuals right to life, liberty and property.

AIMS AND OBJECTIVES

In line with its founding principles, the International Freedom Foundation is pursuing the following goals:

(a) Promoting the concept of free and open societies based on the principles of the free market.

(b) Advancing the theme of freedom, while recognising and respecting the sovereignty and cultural heritage of free nations.

(c) Consolidating support for freedom fighters in their struggle for liberty and democracy.

(d) Mobilising support for reformist societies, especially where the prospects for the movement towards greater freedom are threatened by the forces of terrorism and violent revolution.

(e) Creating forums for dialogue and discussion in an increasingly constrained international environment, where uniformity and sloganising is mistaken for freedom of expression and free thought.

BRANCHES

The Head Office of the International Freedom Foundation is situated in Washington D.C. because the scope and orientation of the Foundation is global, it is in the process of opening branch offices throughout the world. Branch Offices already in operation include:

LONDON, to reach the people of Western Europe and to address the problems of freedom and security on a divided continent.

JOHANNESBURG, to analyse the constantly changing face of Southern Africa, where the forces of freedom are trying to develop new social structures in the face of determined outside aggression.

As resources permit, the Foundation hopes to open branches in Central America, The Middle East and East Asia, other regions in the forefront of the struggle for freedom.

SPONSORSHIP
The International Freedom Foundation is supported by voluntary donations from individuals, corporations and foundations, and from the sale of its publications, internationally.

The International Freedom Foundation accepts no governmental funds and maintains its total independence from government entities.

INTERNATIONAL CHAIRMAN
Jack Abramoff

HEAD OFFICE
International Freedom Foundation (USA)
200 G Street, NE
Suite 300
Washington, DC 20002
United States of America   (202) 546-5788

BRANCHES
International Freedom Foundation (UK)
10 Storey's Gate
London
SW1 3AY   (01) 600-0584

International Freedom Foundation (RSA)
P O Box 67926
Bryanston, 2021
Republic of South Africa   (011) 339-2621/2

Southern Africa

CONTENTS

NOTES

FOREWORD

Rarely a day goes by without a morning newspaper or the evening newscast running a story on South Africa. The issue has, of late, become a preoccupation of many of our churches, universities, think-tanks and lawmakers. Commentaries and analyses abound. Indeed, "South Africa watching" is a growth industry.

Yet it is all so predictable. The reporter shocks us with graphic tales of violence and injustice; the activist, whether he be a churchman or a policy analyst, tells us that something must be done to correct the injustice; and the politician takes to the stump to prescribe the solution - sanctions.

The news consumer sits passively by as his government imposes sanctions. His guilty conscience is assuaged because his country is, after all, doing something to better the lives of black people in Africa - or so he thinks.

In reality, economic sanctions as an instrument of foreign policy rarely, if ever, achieve their intended effect. The sanctioned country, the behavior of which is distasteful or inimical to the sanctioning country, usually finds a way around the sanctions, or simply tightens its belt. And though the application of sanctions allows the sanctioning country to feel good, such application is usually an indication that the sanctioning country lacks any substantive means to influence the target country's behavior.

The champions of sanctions maintain that their strategy is the only tool available to the West to eliminate South Africa's discriminatory system of apartheid. They argue that once the international community completely isolates South Africa - denying that country access to Western capital, technology, goods and export markets - the white minority government will drop to its knees and turn power over to the black majority.

What the pro-sanctions lobby fail to recognise is that apartheid is a dying institution; and that the free market mechanisms of commerce and industry are what is killing it. Sanctions only delay apartheid's final demise by denying black South Africans, through unemployment, hunger and related miseries, the very weapon which will liberate them - economic power. The ultimate demise of apartheid will be found in the creation of more jobs and greater wealth for black South Africans, not in their impoverishment.

As UNDERSTANDING SANCTIONS shows, most black South Africans are aware of this reality. It is only a vocal minority within South Africa's black communities which actually endorses sanctions. And they are allied with those who cold-bloodedly calculate that the man with an empty stomach is more easily turned into a revolutionary.

The reader will learn that to increase the suffering of those already oppressed is neither moral nor desirable. To destroy that which remains of apartheid's collectivist and racist institutions by extending opportunity and freedom to all, irrespective of race, is both.

Jack Abramoff,
International Chairman,
International Freedom Foundation,
WASHINGTON D.C.

INTRODUCTION

'Understanding Sanctions' is the result of a number of years interest in the South African sanctions debate, including two as a parliamentary researcher at Westminster, combined with growing concern at the current direction it is taking. The need for some reference examining the **perceived** rights and wrongs of the sanctions issue, political and economic reality, the effect of sanctions upon South African constitutional and reform processes and, most importantly, the views of black South Africans on the subject is clear.

Researching this work brought home to me, time and time again, how misguided Western politicians, and public/opinion has been over sanctions - particularly regarding where black South African opinion stood. The sheer arrogance of Western European and North American politicians, thousands of miles removed from the situation, deciding what is in the best interests of black South Africans should be clear to anyone. When in addition to ignoring the clearly articulated opinions of millions of South Africa's black citizens, these politicians deem economic suffering, destabilisation and job losses also to be in order, the argument has come a full circle. Is not a key aspect of apartheid the concept of white politicians unilaterally deciding what is or is not in the best interests of blacks?

In addition to providing source material clearly articulating black South African opposition to sanctions and disinvestment, this work also seeks to address a second key inter-related issue. Sanctions would undoubtedly undermine commerce and industry and in doing so would handicap a crucial cog in the anti-apartheid process. Capitalism, and the market mechanism, are sworn enemies of apartheid, and their track record in attacking and helping to dismantle apartheid is a clear one. Far from being hesitant or even ashamed about commercial involvement in South Africa, British, United States and local companies involved in the South African economy should acknowledge the fact that capitalism has mortally wounded apartheid. Commercial involvement in South Africa has done more to destroy apartheid than any number of conferences or street demonstrations in Western Europe. To damage, by means of sanctions and disinvestment, this inherently anti-apartheid commercial pressure weakens the prospects for a peaceful resolution of South Africa's problems.

If this publication succeeds only in making the reader aware of an alternative black South African viewpoint on the sanctions issue, then the author deems it to have been worthwhile. One hopes it goes further and re-asserts the key role which commercial investment has played, and must continue to play, in destroying apartheid in South Africa.

D.H.
London.

Chapter One
THE SANCTIONS DEBATE

1 THE IMMORALITY OF SANCTIONS

The debate surrounding sanctions and South Africa, brought sharply into focus by Margaret Thatcher's adamant rejection of punitive economic measures, and the resultant conflict within the Commonwealth and United Nations, has shown - with the exception of the British prime minister's standpoint - a distinct shortsightedness both in policy and analysis. Visits by Western politicians such as Senator Edward Kennedy and British Labour Party shadow foreign secretary Denis Healey, with their inevitable demand for immediate change in South Africa, coupled to the threat of comprehensive mandatory sanctions if this change was not forthcoming, are typical examples of misplaced and unthought-through Western pressure.

It is difficult to rationalise the fact that South Africa should be punished mid-way through a process of constitutional and political reform. For all the constant recital of what apartheid has meant, the simple fact of the matter is that apartheid as devised and designed by its architects Dr D F Malan and Hendrik Verwoerd (1) in the nineteen fifties and sixties, and as constantly pointed to by people such as Bishop Trevor Huddleston, the British Anti-Apartheid Movement, or Randall Robinson's TransAfrica Group in the United States, no longer functions.

The very essence of apartheid, the "Pass Laws", have been scrapped along with influx control, forced removals and job reservation. Citizenship has been permanently restored to millions of black South Africans. Public amenities have been desegregated, black property rights recognised and the permanency of black urban communities accepted. There is already a system of limited multi-racial local government.

Black trade unions, collective bargaining and the right to strike are now facts of everyday life, as are multi-racial marriages, and the offensive clauses in immigration and immorality legislation have been repealed. Parity for all groups in areas such as education has been agreed upon.

The background to this entire process of political reform was the constitutional referendum result of 1983 - a result which signalled for the first time that white South Africans were willing to share full political rights with their fellow citizens. Although unrecognised by most Western democrats, and deliberately downplayed by those with a vested interest in maintaining an apartheid bogeyman, this volte-face in white opinion was quite an achievement for the Botha administration.

That this willingness has been somewhat dented by the negative Western response to what has been considerable change can now, unfortunately, be seen in the rising tide of white nationalist extremism.

An immediate sign that Western moves towards politically and economically isolating South Africa are fundamentally misguided is that they have been welcomed by both extremes of the political spectrum in that country. Neo-fascist white extremists have embraced isolation for two reasons. It confirms their claim that despite a sincere and sustained attempt at reform, white South Africans have actually been punished by the West. Secondly, this isolation enables them to reject the liberal concept of a grouping of states within Southern Africa as an answer to South Africa's complex ethnic situation, demanding instead the withdrawal into a "siege" mentality, carrying with it a reversion to the Verwoerdian vision of an apartheid-controlled unitary state system.

The evidence to hand is that with each Western snub President Botha, and other reformers such as the liberal Progressive Federal Party, have lost more ground electorally and generally to the overtly racist Herstigte Nasionale Party (HNP), the Conservative Party led by Dr Andries Treurnicht and the militantly pro-apartheid 'Afrikaner Weerstands Beweging' (AWB) of white extremist leader Eugene Terreblanche - so much so that the liberal PFP was ousted as the Official Opposition by the pro-apartheid Conservative Party, itself created as a right-wing backlash to Botha's reforms, in the recent May 1987 general election. Western endeavours to feel good and "do something", however clumsy, are strengthening the hands of those promoting a distinctly neo-fascist tendency in South Africa.

The call for sanctions and South Africa's international isolation has also been welcomed by the equally extreme African National Congress and their ideological mentors, the South African Communist Party. They see disinvestment and sanctions as further damaging an already delicate economy, which in turn will lead to more unemployment, more suffering and more distress amongst the black population of South Africa.

The ANC's vested interest in the resultant unrest is evident: it is unrest which they exploit, deliberately destabilising black South Africans, and then using them as cannon fodder in the "class struggle". The mounting death toll in South Africa's townships is a stark indication of this mentality.

It is therefore an unholy alliance of racists, fascists and Marxists that the West is accommodating in its short-sighted demands for an economic embargo of South Africa.

By far the most relevant dimension of the sanctions debate, however, is that for all the "concern" thus expressed for black South Africans, Western calls for economic sanctions are at odds with clearly stated black wishes. This has been clearly illustrated in various authoritative polls and surveys. The comprehensive London "Sunday Times" opinion poll (August 1986) indicated that a majority of black South Africans were not in favour of sanctions. This poll confirmed the first ever national survey of black worker opinion on the issue. The 1984 Schlemmer Report, commissioned by the United States State Department, indicated an overwhelming 75% rejection of sanctions. Black industrial workers saw foreign commercial involvement as a continuing pressure for positive change and reform.

One prominent black nationalist critic of sanctions and disinvestment is Chief Minister Mangosuthu Buthelezi. A longtime anti-apartheid activist, Buthelezi rejects sanctions, arguing that not only will black poverty and misery be increased but political progress would also be impaired by their imposition. Buthelezi's standpoint is a strong one, outstripping all rivals. His Inkatha liberation movement has one and a third million card-carrying black members. 'United Democratic Front', which the ANC sees as its own creation, has, in comparison an umbrella membership of some 300,000 - many of whom are not black. Buthelezi clearly speaks from a majority black perspective.

Punitive economic measures such as sanctions and disinvestment must be seen as the most misguided and arrogant attempts ever by the international community to punish South Africa. Rather than embarking upon unworkable, unviable and unrealistic sanctions, largely to satisfy the demands of a minority of political extremists sheltering behind the anti-apartheid cloak, Western nations should listen to what moderate, representative black South Africans say on the issue. The danger of Western countries persisting in absent-mindedly pushing for economic disengagement is obvious: these measures play directly into the hands of South Africa's various racial and political extremists, they destabilise black economic and political emancipation, contradict black wishes and endanger the whole Southern African sub-continent.

In appeasing their doctrinaire political pro-sanctions minorities, Western democrats are playing with the lives of all South Africans, black and white. Although by no means a mortal threat to South Africa, the ingredients for violent unrest would be present in some of the possible economic consequences. Why political extremists should desire such a situation is clear: what is disturbing is that this siren call is echoed blindly by governments, organisations and people who should know better.

INTERNATIONAL SANCTIONS AT A GLANCE

	AIR LINKS	KRUGER RANDS	COAL	IRON AND STEEL	URANIUM	AGRICULTURAL PRODUCE	PARASTAL PRODUCE	PETROLEUM	COMPUTER EQUIPMENT	NUCLEAR TRADE	NEW INVESTMENT	PRIVATE LOANS	GOVERNMENT LOANS
		IMPORT BANS						EXPORT BANS			LOANS		
AUSTRALIA	●	●	●	●	●	●		●	●		●V	●V	●
AUSTRIA		●		●				●	●	●	●	●	●
BELGIUM		●		●						●			
BRAZIL								●					
CANADA	●	●V	●	●	●	●		●V				●V	●
DENMARK	●	●	●	●	●	●	●	●	●	●	●		●
FINLAND	●										●	●	●
FRANCE		●	●	●				●		●	●		
GREECE		●		●				●			●		
HOLLAND		●	●V	●	●			●	●	●		●V	●
HONG KONG		●V		●V							●V	●V	●
IRELAND		●		●		●					●		
ISRAEL													
ITALY		●		●							●V		
JAPAN	●	●		●		●			●	●	●	●	●
LUXEMBOURG		●		●							●V		
NEW ZEALAND	●	●	●	●	●	●			●	●		●	●
NORWAY	●	●	●	●	●	●	●	●	●	●	●	●	●
PORTUGAL		●		●						●	●		
SINGAPORE	●	●	●	●	●	●	●	●		●			●
SOUTH KOREA											●	●	●
SPAIN	●	●		●					●		●V		
SWEDEN	●	●	●	●	●	●	●	●	●	●	●	●	●
SWITZERLAND									●	●			●
TURKEY	●				●					●			●
UNITED KINGDOM		●		●				●	●	●	●V		●
UNITED STATES	●	●	●	●	●	●	●	●	●	●	●	●	●
WEST GERMANY		●		●						●	●		

SOURCE: US STATE DEPARTMENT

● = SANCTIONS IN FORCE
V = VOLUNTARY

14

2   THE BACKGROUND TO SANCTIONS

International pressure aimed at isolating the Republic of South Africa from the outside world dates back to the late 1940s, spearheaded by India and raised in forums such as the United Nations. On South Africa's departure from the Commonwealth, and total independence from the United Kingdom, several black African states demanded political and economic sanctions against the new republic.

In early November 1962, the United Nations General Assembly passed a resolution calling for all members to break diplomatic relations with South Africa and to suspend all economic links. This was followed by similar moves in the Organisation of African Unity in June 1963. That year also saw the introduction of United Nations Security Council Resolutions 181/182, effectively banning the supply of all weapons, armaments and military equipment to South Africa - resolutions confirmed by Security Council Resolution 282 in 1970 and made mandatory by the passing of Security Council Resolution 418 in 1977. The United Nations arms embargo was reaffirmed in December 1984.

In March 1965, a United Nations special committee recommended economic sanctions against South Africa. In 1976, the United Nations approved a mandatory oil embargo, echoing a 1973 OPEC embargo. This particular move was blocked by the abstention of Britain, France and the United States. The area of sport with South Africa was embargoed as a result of the 1977 Commonwealth Gleneagles Agreement, effectively excluding South African sportsmen and women from international competition.

The United States ceased all South African Export-Import Bank loans as early as 1964, and moved to block International Monetary Fund purchases of South African gold. A recent development in the attempt to isolate South Africa internationally has been the disinvestment campaign. This has seen both Western national and local government pressure being brought to bear on multinationals and institutions. This pressure has taken two forms. One has been attempts to force multinationals to withdraw investments from the South African economy, and another has been to coerce institutions, especially pension funds, to withdraw investments in companies involved in South Africa. In both these instances there has been considerable legislation brought into play aimed at enforcing these sanctions. There has also been considerable private sector pressure to disinvest.

The Table of voluntary and mandatory sanctions against South Africa on Page 14 was compiled by the US State Department

3 SANCTIONS DO NOT WORK

One of the particularly salient arguments in regard to the sanctions debate is that sanctions patently have not, and do not work. A recent study "Economic Sanctions Reconsidered" by Gary Clyde Hufbauer and Jeffrey Schott of the Institute for International Economics concludes in the words of the 'Economist' that in seeking to resolve political disputes by the use of economic sanctions, governments were "more often than not wasting their time". Two points which the study brought out are that with the exception of wartime measures, the only example of a successful use of punitive economic measures for "major policy aims" was the Arab oil embargo during the early seventies. The study examined the use of sanctions in 108 cases since 1914: in only 39 examples could progress towards a stated goal be claimed because of economic pressure. The ideal target, the study states, is a weak friend: South Africa may be pro-Western but it cannot be labelled as a weak nation.

Even the example of Rhodesia runs contrary to this general rule of thumb. International mandatory and comprehensive economic sanctions were in force against the Rhodesian administration from 1965 to 1980: these patently failed to bring that regime to its knees - despite the fact that its simple economy was heavily linked to that of the United Kingdom. With the developed sector of the Rhodesian economy at one-twentieth of that of South Africa's natural resources and a communications infrastructure hardly developed in comparison with South Africa, Rhodesia defied punitive economic measures, trading illegally with at least sixty countries, including several in the Far East, Latin America, the Third World, and even the Soviet Bloc. The lesson for attempting to enforce the same mandatory comprehensive sanctions upon South Africa are very clear indeed.

4 SANCTIONS VIOLATE BASIC FREEDOMS

From a purely freedom-orientated perspective, leaving aside for a moment the issue of whether or not black South Africans actually support the concept of punitive economic measures against the South African economy, the mandatory imposition of sanctions at a national or local level is morally unfounded. If individuals wish to engage in an economic embargo against anyone else, that is their right. As the South African economist Leon Louw puts it:

"Voluntary sanctions by anyone, against anyone, anywhere, for any reason are consistent with free enterprise...From a free market point of view, if a multinational decides to invest in, or withdraw from, South

Africa voluntarily, its decision is legitimate regardless of how much one might disagree with their reasons." (2)

What becomes totally unacceptable is any form of state coercion, be it at a national or local level, aimed at preventing individuals or companies from investing where they see fit. Such unwarranted governmental interference is in the same category as exchange control or protectionism - government intervention in economic activity. Almost every Western nation has introduced some level of legislation outlawing all or selected areas of economic activity involving South Africa. Examples of this enforced governmental interference include the state of Massachusetts in the United States, where the chief investment officer of state pension funds estimated that Massachusetts lost $14.4 million in four months because of the state disinvestment laws. (3) The contradiction in governments such as those of Margaret Thatcher and Ronald Reagan, based as solidly as they are on free market values, being party to economic intervention is a clear one:

"(I)t is curious that at no time in the international sanctions debate have conservative or liberal groups objected solely on the grounds that government imposed sanctions would be an unwarranted interference in the economy and economic freedom of the country concerned." (4)

Chapter Two
SANCTIONS SUPPORT APARTHEID

The international pro-sanctions/disinvestment lobby, including both the Marxist and reformist left, appears to suffer from two main illusions with regard to the South African economy. The first is that South Africa's apartheid system (the political 'superstructure') has been constructed upon, and serves the interests of, free enterprise capitalism (the economic 'base'). By undermining the latter, the argument follows, the former will collapse.

The second contention is that externally imposed sanctions will contribute to a collapse of the South African economy and to mounting domestic political conflict. A consequence of this, the argument goes, will be that South African capitalists, and the white community in general, will come to accept the inevitability of majority rule and will see this as desirable when compared to total chaos and decline.

1 The First Fallacy

"Apartheid as a system is based upon the free enterprise system"

The apartheid system is not the inevitable product of capitalist logic, but, on the contrary, represents the triumph of politics over economics, as Professor Hutt commented in his book 'The Politics of the Colour Bar' nearly twenty years ago. If institutionalised racial discrimination was indeed intimately linked to the existence of the free enterprise system, why is it the case that apartheid does not exist in all societies which can be characterised as capitalist?

Apartheid structures in South Africa (as in the southern states of America until the mid-1960s) have been imposed by successive governments utilising the full coercive power of the state to regulate and alter the behaviour of individuals from what it would otherwise be. Market economics based upon private ownership of the means of production, and voluntary exchange and interaction between individual producers and consumers, represent the direct antithesis of the type of state intervention represented by apartheid, as well as by all other collectivist systems of government.

It is interesting to note that racial discrimination and enforced separation is practiced in those areas of life controlled by the South African state - schools, hospitals, residential areas and still - in some places - transport and local amenities such as public swimming pools. In contrast, very few private establishments and institutions, including restuarants, retail outlets, schools, hospitals, hotels, theatres, clinics and sports stadiums practice racialism. Why is this?

18

2 The market is 'colour blind'

The answer is that racial discrimination carries with it high costs for entrepreneurs. A trader who turns away a potential customer because he is of a particular ethnic origin will forgo his financial patronage. The victim of discrimination will then take his purchasing power to a non-discriminatory outlet, which will gain as a result. Most employers want to hire workers who are efficient and competitive in terms of the wages they are prepared to work for. Colour of skin does not come into it. A racialist boss may well find he is obliged to take on less efficient and more expensive staff simply to satisfy his prejudices. The vast majority of traders - racialist, sexist, ageist or whatever - are not prepared to lose money in this way. Capitalism, unlike statism, is thus a great equaliser. This is what Hutt meant when he talked of the market being 'colour blind'.

Contrary to popular myth, the arrival of whites in South Africa did not herald the birth, and imposition, of capitalism. Instead, it resulted in the coercive destruction of exchange networks that were already in place, and in the confiscation, and subsequent redistribution of private agricultural land and livestock that originally belonged to indigenous farmers. The various land acts passed in the nineteenth and twentieth centuries, culminating in the 1913 Native Land Act, were such examples. Professor Hutt stated in his work that the mix of racial discrimination and socialism that came to be known as apartheid was the product of democratic government - albeit restricted to whites only - **not** the result of its absence. A coalition of white interests was able to gain control of the state apparatus, through the electoral process, in order to then impose policies which were in their self-interest - but which were contrary to the economic advancement of blacks and the white business community. The lesson Hutt drew from his observation of racial socialism in South Africa was that government should not merely be representative in a democratic sense but **limited** as well, through the use of constitutional devices. These devices, in limiting the scope for state action, would help to protect the rights of the individual.

3 Apartheid equals racialism plus socialism

White, English-speaking workers organised in the trade union movement, and the South African Labour Party, together with poor, unskilled Afrikaners, succeeded in getting successive administrations to introduce legislation designed to rig the labour market in favour of themselves. Hence the passing of the Colour Bar Act, which restricted the number of blacks that could be employed in the mines; the Wages Act of 1925, which, by stipulating a 'standard rate' for the job, in effect priced many blacks out of the market; the various Job Reservation Acts; the infamous Pass laws which required blacks to have a permit to live in an urban area and so sought to control the movement and quantity of labour (just as in the socialist Eastern Bloc countries): and many other repressive, anti-free market statutes. Apartheid was also of course extended to the cultural sphere. Parliamentary acts followed relating to inter-racial marriage, to the creation of separate living areas for people of different colours, and to separate social amenities.

These racialistically motivated measures have not only been an affront to the principle of personal liberty in its broadest sense, but have also placed restrictions on an individual's economic choices. Whites are forbidden from selling their houses to non-whites because of the Group Areas Act; blacks have been denied the opportunity to set up shop in white designated business areas (and vice versa), and so forth. In addition to a plethora of racial controls of the type described above, the South African economy has also been subjected to a high degree of collectivistic intervention. A higher proportion of South African industries are under state ownership than in any of the Scandinavian social democracies. The railways, airways, telecommunications and harbours are all in the public sector. Agricultural produce must be marketed and sold through state-controlled agricultural control boards. A very significantly sized bureaucracy and high rate of taxation have also come into being. Far from being an example of market capitalism, South Africa has all the characteristics of a highly collectivist mixed economy. For black people, however, the degree to which their lives are subjected to government regulation is even greater. The outlets they can shop from are, in effect, local monopolies because of state licensing policy. The schools their children go to are in the public sector, as are the local health services. Travel (with the exception of taxis) to and from work is also by courtesy of public trains and buses.

4 Capitalism is destroying Apartheid

The healthy desire to make profits means that businessmen have probably more of an incentive to undermine apartheid, in its economic and cultural manifestations, than any other sector in the South African community. It is worth recalling, with direct reference to the sanctions debate, that opposition to racial discrimination in the economic sphere gathered momentum among white capitalists a long time before moves to isolate the Republic were initiated. The business community has always given the bulk of its support to political parties opposed to state-enforced separation. As American political commentator Merle Lipton has pointed out in 'Capitalism and Apartheid'(1), the changing structure of the domestic economy has intensified capitalist opposition to the status quo. This has been in part because of the growing numbers of Afrikaans speakers moving into the business world. Secondly, the decline in the significance of mining and agriculture (which relied upon cheap and unskilled labour forces) and the increasing dependence of the country on manufacturing and services have also played their part. Modern managers in these expanding sectors require skilled black labour capable of using increasingly sophisticated machinery. The statutory exclusion of non-whites from certain types of employment and positions clearly provided an obstacle to the development of capital. The need of South African manufacturers to break into foreign markets because of the small size of the domestic market, makes changes that will facilitate competitiveness all the more important.

Thus, the pro-sanctions lobby, by attempting to weaken the South African economy, are also weakening that sector of South African society most committed to destroying apartheid - the small, medium and large-scale businessman. If an effective attempt was made at imposing sanctions and disinvestment upon South Africa, the state would be forced to intervene in order to structure the response to this outside challenge. This would immediately result in an even larger degree of state intervention in the economy than at present - and would considerably narrow the role for private businessmen and entrepreneurs, hence denying them a greater role in attacking apartheid itself.

5 The Second Fallacy

"The decline of the South African economy provides the best prospect for an end to the system of apartheid"

The African National Congress (ANC) and their socialist supporters in the outside world, desire sanctions and disinvestment because they believe these measures will precipitate an economic collapse, resulting in a violent overthrow of the "unreformable" apartheid state, or at least, in its unconditional surrender.

If, for the sake of argument, it is accepted that sanctions will precipitate economic decline, and that this, in turn, will result in the doomsday scenario envisaged, then surely this, in itself, should provide Western democrats with a good reason for vociferously opposing the imposition of sanctions. It is bewildering to many moderate South Africans that so many Westerners, who profess a commitment to liberal values, are, at one and the same time prepared to align themselves so closely with the demands of anti-democratic elements within their own countries. As Chief Buthelezi has put it:

"Americans who support the politics of non-violence and of negotiation should therefore ask themselves why America should support disinvestment when, within South Africa, it is championed solely by those who seek to establish a non-capitalist state through the use of violence" (2)

However, the belief that economic depression will fuel the flames of Marxist insurrection is based upon a characteristically unrealistic assessment, on the part of the far left, of the relative balance of forces within South Africa. These include the very deep political divisions that exist within the non-white communities, the vast military resources at the disposal of the South African state, and the deep commitment of the vast majority of white South Africans to prevent a Marxist takeover at any cost.

Instead, two different contentions are presented here. The first is that, if it is indeed the case that sanctions or disinvestment produce the malignant economic consequences that it is claimed they do, the most likely beneficiaries will be those white political movements opposed to change in a liberal direction, and desirous of a reimposition of those repressive racialist measures that have been repealed within the past decade or so. The second is that the expansion of the domestic economy and, in particular, the development of a large, non-white, property-owning class, and a materially prosperous black workforce, offers the best prospect of creating a political environment in which liberal reform is likely to succeed.

6 Sanctions Undermine Reform

Mass black unemployment and impoverishment resulting in street riots, an increase in violent crime, and enhanced support for extreme Soviet-backed organisations is not a climate in which white South Africans, liberal or otherwise in sympathy, are likely to favour progressive constitutional change, including an extension of the franchise to include all ethnic communities. The recent political histories of most African countries do not provide white South African voters with a very optimistic picture of a likely outcome of majority rule. The saying "One Man, One Vote - Once" is ingrained in the minds of many white South Africans. In particular, the hand-over of power in neighbouring Zimbabwe, and the subsequent blood-stained drift of that country towards a Marxist one-party state under Robert Mugabe's leadership (combined with the introduction of even more draconian curbs on political and civil liberties than under the previous Rhodesian Front administration), has served to confirm the worst fears

22

of the minority population concerning democracy's prospect of longevity in the African context. Heightened domestic turbulence and tension make it all the easier for the enemies of reform to persuade the South African electorate that voting to dismantle political apartheid is tantamount to voting for an end to white civilisation, prosperity and political liberties. Civil strife fueled by economic decay also fuels fear and anxiety. Security issues move to the top of the domestic agenda, not reform - a viewpoint underlined by the veteran South African anti-apartheid parliamentarian and activist Helen Suzman, who argues that, for example, the choice facing the government might be spending on the military or black education: "If white survival is in the balance, I have no doubt which priority the government will settle for".(3)

Not surprisingly, most whites do not view the possibility of a transition to a one-party state socialist dictatorship as a desirable prospect, or as a desirable alternative to the present status quo. The vast majority of whites, and a growing percentage of non-whites as well, perceive the totalitarian scenario the ANC/South African Communist Party Alliance has mapped out for South Africa's future as the logical extension and reinforcement of the authoritarian system that already prevails. So long as the choice appears to be the present system, however flawed, versus one man, one vote in a unitary South Africa (with no constitutional restraints on the power of the state) then whites will continue to opt for what they consider to be the lesser of two evils.

7 Power-Sharing Accepted

A survey conducted in 1986 showed that 81 percent of National Party supporters and 93 percent of Progressive Federal Party voters supported and accepted the idea of power sharing with the black majority, so long as there was no "domination". While 41 percent of government supporters accepted voting rights on equal terms with whites, 48 percent said they would only support the extension of the franchise if they did not perceive this as threatening 'white interests'. A surprisingly high 40 percent of ultra right-wing Conservative Party supporters also stated their willingness to accept the dismantling of political apartheid with that proviso.(4) Thus support for reform is clearly a majority position. However, it will only be expressed in politically practical terms if it is perceived that a sufficiently large proportion of the various non-white groups adhere to political and economic values similar to those of the minority community. Attempts then to deliberately expand the number of materially impoverished and politically disaffected black people will prove highly counter-productive in terms of trying to persuade white South Africans to pressurise their government to speed up the reform process.

23

8 A misguided Western approach

Those Western politicians, such as Congressman Stephen Solarz of the United States, who believe that the best way to bring about constitutional change is to deliberately promote conflict within South Africa have seriously misread the South African situation and are sadly ignorant of the mass psychology of the white community.

A refutation of the Solarz model of change is, arguably, shown by reference to the fact that the Verwoerdian Conservative Party achieved by far its best election results during the general election of 6 May 1987, in the Northern Transvaal, an area of the country in which terrorist activity, in terms of the laying of landmines and attacks on isolated farm houses, has been the most prevalent. By contrast, there is negligible support for white supremicist policies in those places which have had little or no experience of mass unrest and terrorist activity - the Western Cape, Orange Free State and Natal provinces of South Africa.

9 Natal, the way forward?

Natal provides a good example of the type of conditions in which white support for reform can be gained. Traditionally, in this province relations between individuals of all races have been peaceful. A more relaxed atmosphere has persisted throughout the province than in many other parts of South Africa. Natal is the home of the Zulu nation, who constitute the largest single part of the country's black population. A clear majority of Zulus support the 1.3 million strong black Inkatha movement, South Africa's largest political organisation led by Chief Buthelezi. The movement's principles were described by him as being a commitment to:

"(T)he rule of law in an open, race-free society and for progress through the responsible development of free enterprise. It rejects violence as the best means of bringing about radical change in South Africa, and is committed to non-violent tactics and strategies, to the politics of negotiation. It stands, in other words, for the very things which America epitomises" (5)

It is surely no coincidence that in the province of Natal the overwhelming majority of whites enthusiastically support an end to political apartheid. Polls have shown also that Natal whites would be happy to see Chief Buthelezi become the political leader of the province.

Outside of Natal, information concerning the opinions of black people is patchy. Polls and studies have shown very different and contradictory attitudes towards free enterprise. At present, most whites are sceptical as to the commitment of blacks to political tolerance and economic liberties. If this view is an accurate assessment of black sentiment it can hardly be said to be surprising. Non-whites have not been encouraged, or given the opportunity to participate in Western-style democratic structures or to develop entrepreneurial skills by successive South African governments. How then can the majority now be expected to defend political structures and economic processes that they were excluded from for so long?

10 Economic de-regulation will speed reform

The urgent need now is for those opposed to apartheid, both within, and outside, South Africa, to agitate for the quick introduction of measures which will facilitate an increase in support for liberal values. A crucial component of any meaningful reform package must be the wholesale de-regulation of the South African economy. Black South Africans must be presented with a window of economic opportunity. The power of white bureaucrats to deny black entrepreneurs the sites and the licenses they need to operate must be removed. At present would-be black businessmen not only face the discouraging thicket of regulations that all South Africans have to contend with, but in addition, can be denied the opportunity to trade simply because the white controlled agencies can decide there is no "need and desirability" for certain types of outlets. As a consequence of this depth of stifling control, townships like Soweto probably have fewer retail outlets per capita than anywhere outside of the Eastern Bloc. As leading South African free-market economist Leon Louw has put it:

"South African blacks today have no experience of law which is equally applicable to all regardless of sex, creed or colour. What they experience now, from day to day, is arbitary rule by men, a system which by its nature is rife with both real and suspected corruption. No self-respecting human being can be subjected to such a system without feeling frustrated or angry"   (6)

11 Free the informal sector

De-regulation will enable the development of a prosperous 'second logic' economic sector, to use the Anglo-American Corporation economist Clem Sunter's phrase. This being informal to small and medium sized enterprises utilising medium to low technologically productive methods, as opposed to the high tech, research and capital intensive 'first logic' sector. The latter sphere will not be capable, on its own, of generating the additional wealth and employment that South Africa needs to develop in

25

order to meet the requirements of a rapidly expanding population. The second logic economy provides, Sunter believes, the best prospects of securing the bulk of new employment and higher standards for South Africans. But it is precisely this area of economic activity which is most vulnerable to excessive state regulations. Big, established corporations may be able to live with burdensome controls, but small businesses on the margin of profitability rarely can. Many potential businessmen fail to emerge in the first place because the disincentives are too great to begin with. South Africa needs a "...system of government that supports small entrepreneurs and gives them the freedom to flourish".(7) One relevant case study could be the present administration's imaginative decision to de-regulate taxi travel, and so to effectively break the state monopoly on transport for black South Africans: this was an important step in the right direction and shows what can be achieved. There are now hundreds of thousands of black taxi owners throughout the country; individuals for whom the prospect of a Soviet-style South Africa "in which all transport will be organised by the authorities" is a good deal less attractive than it might have been a few years ago.

12   Towards wider black share-ownership

Another positive step genuine anti-apartheid activists should encourage is the move to provide South African workers with shares, so as to give them a real stake in their companies and in the future prosperity of the country. In November 1987, both the Ford Motor Company and the Anglo-American Corporation launched schemes to facilitate black employees' equity participation. Movement towards a property-owning democracy would also be assisted by a radical privatisation programme, in which perhaps 50 percent of the shares in each state-owned corporation to be returned to the private sector would be set aside at generous rates for black South Africans.

By utilising these, and other mechanisms, the hope must be that an expanding base of support for liberal values can be created amongst the majority population. Once this has taken root throughout the country, then the type of support for political reform that has already been secured among whites in Natal will be replicated nationally.

CONCLUSION

It should be clear from this brief examination of sanctions and disinvestment - their interaction with the capitalist market economy and the free enterprise argument itself - that far from speeding up the process of dismantling what remains of apartheid, sanctions and the effects of sanctions upon the South African economy, upon South African businessmen and upon economic de-regulation, would be very harmful indeed. Far from being punished, South African entrepreneurs should be encouraged as much as possible.

A positively charged economy would see the increasing emergence of black entrepreneurs with a share in the future of South Africa. This, in turn, would lead to more black consumer power which would be able to force more and more concessions in, if nothing else, the economic field, but, also very probably within the political arena. A strong, economically rooted and active black middle class, sharing many of the same values and goals as white South Africans, would provide a very suitable seedbed indeed for positive negotiation between South Africa's various communities.

An economically disrupted South Africa would be a South Africa full of domestic unrest, fuelled by thousands of black South Africans - the first victims of sanctions - with no stake in the future of anything; people who would become the ideological cannon fodder for those organisations such as the African National Congress and South African Communist Party, committed to a violent overthrow of South African society and to the establishment of a Marxist one-party state. Domestic conflict would also serve the interests of those committed to an equally unacceptable solution - those fascist and neo-fascist white supremacists, as characterised by far-right leader Eugene Terreblanche. To them international isolation serves to force South Africa into an uncompromising siege mentality. The domestic turmoil caused by economic suffering as the result of sanctions - despite the National Party's already promulgated, undreamed of political concessions - would be their ideal arguments for abandoning totally the concept of reform or power-sharing and returning to the doctrinaire Verwoerdian concept of apartheid.

Chapter Three
THE EFFECTS OF SANCTIONS

There can be no doubt whatsoever that the economic link between the Republic of South Africa and the Western industrialised nations is both an exceedingly valuable and strategic one. Depite the fact that the disinvestment and sanctions campaigns have been active since the 1960s, investment by, and economic interactions between the Western democracies and South Africa have increased. Foreign investment, for example, has increased from some R23 billion in 1979 to a 1986 level of more than R43 billion: accounting for one tenth of all investment in South Africa itself.(1) On a similar level, the relationship between South Africa and her neighbours in Southern Africa is, if anything, even closer. This chapter seeks to examine the simple, black on white possible effects of a concerted disinvestment and/or sanctions campaign against South Africa on Western Europe/North America, Britain, South Africa and Southern Africa. A section also briefly examines the strategic mineral lifeline which would be severed in the event of effective economic sanctions.

1 WESTERN EUROPE

The West German-based Institute for European Economic Studies, in association with the French Ecole Superieure de Commerce and the Fachhochschule of West Germany, three major European business study centres, published their findings with regard to the possible Western price tag on implementing sanctions against and disinvesting from South Africa:

"For all European Community countries, an embargo of trade with South Africa would cost about 330,000 jobs. If the US were to join such action, the number would increase by 122,000 jobs. With Japanese exports included, the Western world might lose 500,000 jobs if an embargo against South Africa was imposed" (2)

There is no doubt that most Western industrialised nations would be hit in some way by punitive economic measures. Even a country such as Sweden, which has for almost a decade attempted to distance itself economically from South Africa, would feel the effects of Western European sanctions on South Africa. Mr Bengt-Erik Nilsson, an executive of Sweden's War Contingency, Strategical and Psychological Authority has warned, for example, that large sections of Swedish industry would be adversely affected.

28

2 THE UNITED KINGDOM

The effects of a concerted sanctions/disinvestment campaign on Britain and British employment would be multifacetted. This much is at least tacitly agreed upon by most of the major political parties. The British-South African relationship, based on family, historical and economic links, is a strong one. United Kingdom exports to South Africa concentrate on heavy engineering and mining equipment, transport, and farming equipment. Approximately ten percent of all British overseas investment is in South Africa. The 1982 figure of some £11,000 million of direct British overseas investment in South Africa is still applicable. (3)

The United Kingdom South Africa Trade Association Estimate of Job Losses:

The United Kingdom South Africa Trade Association (UKSATA), an organisation representing some 300 British firms involved in trade with South Africa, warned as early as 1978 about the costs to Britain of any punitive economic measures against South Africa:

"(I)ncreased unemployment estimated at 70,000 would result in Britain, since alternative markets for many of these exports are simply not available"

If an economic boycott hampered imports of South African products, then this denial of:

"(T)he supply of vital raw materials imported from South Africa, most of which could not be readily replaced even at increased cost from other sources... would probably result in a huge rise in unemployment (of) perhaps as much as 180,000..." (4)

UKSATA therefore estimated that some 250,000 British jobs were at risk: 180,000 from the loss of South African import materials and 70,000 from the loss of British exports.

Much of the UKSATA data is the result of CBI surveys of British industry during the 1970s, additional surveys of companies involved in South Africa, and two further surveys. (5)

The original UKSATA figures have been restated by UKSATA in November 1985 (6), and by the Confederation of British Industry in December 1985 (7).

British Government Figures

The British government has cited several figures, based on Department of Trade and Industry statistics, with regard to possible British job losses in connection with sanctions/disinvestment. A figure of 120,000-150,000 is the result of British government calculations on the subject - calculations linked to exports per se.

Mrs Margaret Thatcher, speaking at Prime Minister's question time in Parliament in June 1983 declared that: "there would be 150,000 jobs at stake" if Britain cut its commercial links with South Africa. (8) Three years later, in 1986, she still believed that a high number of Britons, some 120,000 people could lose their employment if sanctions were introduced against South Africa. (9)

British Foreign Secretary, Sir Geoffrey Howe, in testimony to both the House of Commons Foreign Affairs Committee (10), and when speaking during a debate on South Africa in the House in June 1986, stated that 120,000 British jobs were at risk. (11)

3 THE UNITED STATES AND SOUTH AFRICA

Although no comprehensive analysis has been made to date, evidence available points to a significant impact on the United States in the wake of sanctions against South Africa.

According to the October 1987 Investor Responsibility Research Centre's "US and Canadian Business in South Africa 1987" report, there are currently 168 United States companies with direct investment or employees in South Africa - direct investment being defined as a company owning ten percent or more of an active South African subsidiary or affiliate. There are a further 109 American companies cited whose involvement with South Africa is indirect, ie through contracts, licensing, franchising and other agreements with companies in South Africa. Both categories of companies include everything from mining and manufacturing to chemicals and cosmetics.

A total of 131 United States companies have left South Africa since 1984. Ninety-four of these left in 1986 and 1987, primarily in response to the various disinvestment initiatives at local, state and federal level. An additional fourteen companies had announced their intention to leave as of October 1987. With the passage in late December 1987 of legislation eliminating tax credits for US companies doing business in South Africa it is likely that several more will withdraw in the coming months.

Despite United States corporate investment in South Africa accounting for only about one-half of one percent of all US foreign investment, or about $1.2 billion, the United States stands to lose significantly from the imposition of sanctions. In June 1986 the US Department of Commerce prepared a study for the US State Department's South Africa Advisory Committee entitled: "Economic Impact of US Disinvestment from South Africa". The study examines three potential scenarios: continued gradual withdrawal, politically induced mass exit and a Congressionally-mandated withdrawal.

If the withdrawal were orderly - a scenario the report calls "the best of circumstances":

* Some $120 million in foreign exchange will be lost annually to the United States
* ... at least $400 million will be lost annually in foregone export sales; and another $600 million in 'associated' exports will be in jeopardy
* Some 14,000 jobs will be lost as a result of the lost export sales; another 21,000 jobs will be at risk if associated sales were lost as well.

Under the worst of cases, to the above would be added:

* The US firms will lose the proceeds of the sale of their assets in South Africa ... that loss could reach $7.2 billion
* United States firms will be prohibited from collecting the amounts still outstanding on the intercompany loan account, due to likely foreign exchange controls.

The Commerce Department study did not examine the effect on employment and trade figures in the case of a total two-way trade embargo with the United States. It also did not mention the unintended effects of sanctions for US firms, effects such as the possible loss of competitiveness for major international contracts due to unreliability or the United States' loss of reliability as a trading partner because of political considerations dictating policy.

By way of example, it is useful to look at the state of California because its economy is nearly as diverse as that of the United States as a whole. Most of California's industries consume the minerals cobalt, chromium, manganese, platinum and vanadium in some form. Should access to these critical materials be restricted, 58% of California's total manufacturing, or some 1.1 million jobs would be at risk.

American disinvestment terminates black welfare projects

One of the immediate results of Western, and particularly American disinvestment from South Africa has been the termination of large numbers of social projects aimed at improving the conditions of the black community and securing fundamental change in South Africa. Many of the businesses and firms which have cut and run have left behind them a tangled mess of community, social and welfare programmes. The role played by American industrial muscle in liberalising South Africa was a distinct one, as Dr Jan Steyn of the Urban Foundation made clear:

"We found leadership in the United States business community; strong and sensible allies in our efforts, for instance, to secure full property

31

rights for Blacks and to lobby for a positive urbanisation strategy"(12)

The termination of the abovementioned black social welfare programmes and projects by disinvesting United States companies has been criticised by black business leaders such as David Mailoane, executive director of the Soweto Chamber of Commerce:

"We're not happy to see US companies go. But we're even less happy about the manner in which most of them have chosen to leave."(13)

4 POSSIBLE EFFECTS ON SOUTH AFRICA

Because the South African economy is an open economy, reliant on financial interaction, punitive economic measures would undoubtedly have a serious effect on both imports and exports - an effect which could no doubt be contained, but which would be certain to equally manifest itself in job losses.

South Africa's economic linkage to the Western industrialised world is comprehensive. Account for R6.2 billion on 1985 trade figures, the United States was South Africa's largest trading partner: Japan follows with R5.1 billion, West Germany (R5.1 billion), and then the United Kingdom (R4.9 billion). The European Economic Community taken as a whole, however, accounts for the largest share of South African trade; West Germany, Britain, The Netherlands, Italy, France and Belgium all feature in South Africa's top ten trading partners. (12)

According to an extensive study published in July 1986 by the University of South Africa's Bureau of Market Research, some one million South Africans stand to lose jobs in the face of comprehensive trade sanctions. (15) Eighty-four percent of the job losses would be black. The results were based on a scientific survey, checked against secondary sources of more than 3,300 companies employing 52 percent of all employees.

There are already an estimated 1.7 million black South Africans either unemployed or underemployed. Comprehensive trade sanctions would mean 600,000 further black job losses, resulting in 31.9% of all economically active black South Africans being unemployed.

The survey also touched on the crucial importance of job creation within South Africa. Professor Piet Nel, of UNISA's Bureau of Market Research, found that at least 3.6 million jobs will have to be created in South Africa by the turn of the century. For blacks to attain parity in employment with whites, some 6.8 million new employment opportunities will have to be found. All this against a backdrop that the past five years has seen the creation of only 226,000 jobs. The position where employment equalled population growth was only achieved during one ten year period, 1960-70, when South Africa averaged a 5.9% economic growth:

"Thus the real rate of increase in economic activity will have to be extremely rapid if sufficient jobs are to be assured. To this end, enormous sums will have to be invested in the South African economy"(16)

The Institute for European Economic Studies supports the view that job creation is a crucial challenge for the South African economy. Their study of Southern African economics concludes that about 300,000 new job opportunities will have to appear annually in order to accommodate those South Africans coming on to the employment market.

There are an estimated 1,200 British companies active in South Africa, employing some 350,000 workers. Over four hundred and fifty companies of which some one hundred and eighty are major concerns, were identified by British trade authorities in 1981. The British Department of Trade and Industry revealed that some 66 British subsidiaries employed 500 or more South African workers; ten employed more than 5,000 and three employed more than 10,000 people - the ten largest companies employing a combined 100,000 workers in South Africa.(17) More than 300 American companies, including a large percentage of the 100 largest corporations in the United States have subsidiaries or affiliates in the country: six thousand more work through agencies.(18)

Embargo calculations

A 1982 Institute for European Economic Studies projection of losses, based on a possible 20 percent economic embargo alone, calculated that South Africa's exports would have been dropped by about R3,000 million - which would have resulted in unemployment for approximately 440,000 South Africans - 99,000 white and 350,000 black workers.(19)

5 THE QUESTION OF STRATEGIC MINERALS

One point consistently ignored by those who urge a mandatory, total economic embargo of South Africa is that such measures would cut the Western nations' lifeline to crucial strategic minerals - either by prohibiting the import of South African metals and minerals or by freezing the traditional South African export routes for Zairean, Zambian and Zimbabwean strategic metals, as any embargo would do. The danger of Western industrial and military technology suffering as a result is a very real one. Not always naturally endowed with large natural or stockpiled reserves of strategic minerals, the West must always look towards supplier nations in the Third World. Fewer and fewer of these countries either identify with, or are prepared to provide these minerals to Western industrialised states. In any instance, to build up a reliance on Soviet bloc suppliers is at best a hazardous pastime.

With the importance of a secure supply of strategic minerals in mind, Southern Africa's proven reserves should be seen as crucial to the economic, security and military capability, and hence stability, of the Western democracies. In 1986 the Republic of South Africa provided an average of just under one third of the West's requirements for 25 strategic minerals. (20)

CHROMIUM

A crucial strategic mineral, chromium is widely used in the chemical, refractory and metallurgical industries: stainless steel, for example, irreplacable in several vital processes, has a high chromium content. Chromium alloys are also widely used in defence industries - weapons systems, aircraft, ships, naval vessels and missiles. The United States has no reserves of this mineral, and most other Western nations also rely on imports. South Africa is a crucial supplier to the West, matched only by the Soviet Union. South Africa has some 66 percent of all world reserves, and Zimbabwe almost 33 percent. The United States has had to increase its chrome imports from the Soviet Union from an average of 479 tons per month during 1981-5, to an estimated 6,440 tons per month (as of March 1987).(21) Hardly the wisest of security dependencies.

MANGANESE

This mineral is vital to the production of iron and steel - these two metals, in turn, provide the backbone of industrial society. The West has no commercially viable reserves of manganese, and South Africa is the leading supplier of manganese to Western industry. As with chromium, a large proportion of world manganese reserves are to be found in Southern Africa. Soviet reserves match South African deposits but are very seldom made available to Western industry, being used internally or within the Soviet bloc. A 1985 United States Bureau of Mines report warned that "serious consequences would result from a prolonged cut off of supply from the Republic of South Africa".(22)

VANADIUM

Unavailable within the West, classified as a strategic and critical material by the United States, and stock-piled since 1980, vanadium has essential uses within the defence, transport, construction and energy sectors of industry. The world's major supplier of both vanadium slag and ores, with an annual production of some 14,000 tons, is the Republic of South Africa. Again, as with manganese, South African output is equalled by the Soviet Union - Soviet consumption being exclusively domestic. South Africa has around one-fifth of the world vanadium reserves.

PLATINUM RELATED METALS
Because of platinum's essential catalyst functions, its use in electrical circuits, contacts, and fuels, it is of critical importance to modern industry. Amongst the rarest of the metallic elements, the six closely related metals platinum, palladium, rhodium, ruthenium, iridium and osmium are to be found in the Soviet Union, Canada and South Africa. South Africa and the Soviet Union accounted for some 93 percent of world production in 1985. South Africa also has the world's largest proven reserves of these precious metals.

URANIUM
Vital to the ever increasing nuclear industry, uranium is a strategic mineral essential to the West. South Africa is the second largest producer of uranium in the world, after Canada, supplying just over 14 percent of Western output. The Organisation for Economic Co-operation and Development (OECD) has estimated that South African uranium production is worth some US$ 430 million annually.

INDUSTRIAL DIAMONDS
The United States, the world's largest market for industrial diamonds, classifies industrial diamonds as a strategic mineral and stockpiles against any possible disruption. Some 85 percent of all the world's industrial and gem diamonds are marketed by South Africa. Botswana, South Africa and Zaire account for some seventy percent of diamonds mined in the world annually.

COBALT
Zambia and Zaire are the world's leading producers of cobalt, representing some 65 percent of world production in 1985. Other, smaller, quantities are to be found in Botswana, Zimbabwe and South Africa. Used in alloy form in several defence-related industries or as a catalyst, cobalt is a strategic mineral. Almost 75 percent of the West's cobalt reserves are in Zaire and Zambia. Punitive economic sanctions would block export routes for this supply of cobalt.

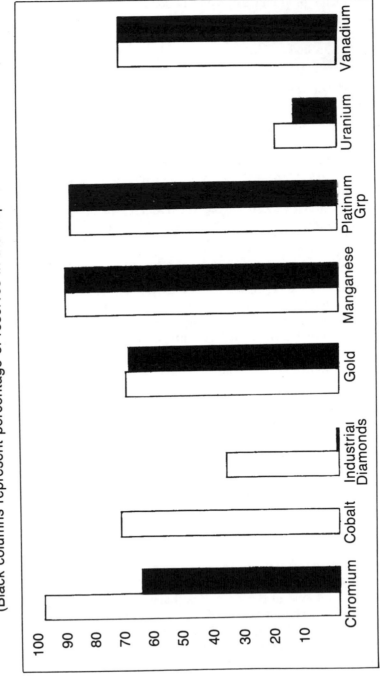

Eight Selected Strategic and Critical Minerals: Percentage of Western Reserves in Southern Africa
(Black columns represent percentage of reserves in the Republic of South Africa)

Of the above minerals all but Gold and Uranium are on the United States Government's stockpiling list

36

GOLD

Almost half the world gold is produced in South Africa. Not only used as a cosmetic commodity and value-guide, gold is essential to quite a number of industrial functions, being used in high-technology, electronics and telecommunications systems. In addition to producing half the world's gold, South Africa also has sixty percent of the world's reserves.

South Africa's share of the West's and the world's mineral reserves

Mineral Commodity	South Africa's Reserves (metric tonnes)	West Rank	West %	World Rank	World %
Manganese Ore (in situ)	12 700 000 000	1	92	1	78
Platinum Group Metals (Metal, 600 m depth)	26 700	1	83	1	70
Gold (Metal)	20 000	1	64	1	51
Chrome Ore (300 m depth)	2 400 000 000	1	57	1	55
Vanadium (Metal), 30 m depth	5 400 000	1	50	1	33
Alumino — Silicates (Ore)	51 600 000	1	47	1	38
Vermiculite (Ore)	73 000 000	2	40	n.a.	n.a.
Diamonds (Gem and Industrial) carats	365 000 000	2	27	2	24
Coal (Bituminous and Anthracite)(Recoverable)	58 404 000 000	2	20	4	11
Antimony (Metal)	254 000	2	12	4	6
Uranium (Metal, up to $US 80/kg U_3O_8)	191 000	2	12	n.a	n.a
Zirconium Minerals (Metal)	6 900 000	3	21	3	18
Fluorspar (Contained CaF_2)	31 000 000	3	11	6	6
Nickel (Metal)	5 480 000	3	11	6	6
Asbestos (Fibre)	7 800 000	3	8	4	6
Phosphates Rock (Contained Concentrates)	2 310 000 000	3	7	3	7
Titanium minerals (Metal)	31 100 000	4	12	4	11
Zinc (Metal)	16 000 000	4	6	4	6
Lead (Metal)	5 400 000	4	5	4	4
Iron Ore	9 400 000 000	5	7	6	5

Note: The mining industry has had significant influence on the development of South Africa's infrastructure with all the consequent benefits for the region as a whole, and its future well-being will be important

6 SOUTHERN AFRICA AND SANCTIONS

In any examination of the effects of sanctions, the possible impact of an economic embargo on Southern Africa as a region cannot be understated. There can be no doubt that comprehensive sanctions against South Africa would have a devasting effect on her regional neighbours. Despite the formation of organisations such as the Southern African Development Co-ordination Council (SADCC), in 1980, with the specific aim of lessening regional dependence on South Africa, the countries of Southern Africa are still critically dependent on the South African economy. The London 'Financial Times' has touched on the dangers inherent in the imposition of sanctions:

"Such is South Africa's dominance of the Southern African economy and so great is the extent of regional interdependence that effective economic sanctions against Pretoria would be bound to have major adverse effects on the front-line states and enclave economies"(23)

COMPARED WITH SOUTHERN AFRICA AS A WHOLE, SOUTH AFRICA ACCOUNTS FOR:

80	percent of the total Gross National Product (1985)
77	percent of the electricity generated (1980)
63	percent of the tarred roads (1982)
60	percent of the railways and harbours (1985)
84	percent of the telephones installed (1977)
80	percent of the motor vehicles (1982)
97	percent of the coal mined (1980)
98	percent of the iron ore mined (1980)
82	percent of the chrome mined (1978)
70	percent of the maize grown (1980)
87	percent of the wheat grown (1980)
67	percent of the sugar cane produced (1979)
39	percent of the cattle flock (1980)
80	percent of the sheep flock (1980)

Source: "Economic Interdependence in Southern Africa", Africa Institute of South Africa, Pretoria 1986.

The adverse direct and indirect effects, regionally, of sanctions against South Africa were also raised in a study of sanctions by Professor Neville Brown and Yu Ying Brown, published in 1987 by the University of Birmingham Graduate School of International Studies:

"(E)ven if there were some punitive measure, economic or whatever that was sharp and decisive in its direct impact; still its indirect effect would ramify unpredictably.

Besides which, any blows aimed at the country are liable to do more damage to certain other Frontline states.

This would apply even if South Africa did not deliberately wage economic warfare against them, if she simply took limited measures to buttress herself." (24)

Trade and Transport

One of the two major areas of direct South African regional interaction is in terms of trade and transport services. South Africa's railways and harbours are of particular importance to its neighbouring states in servicing industrial/commercial interaction. During the 1984/85 financial year the South African Transport Services handled some 6 million tonnes of traffic to and from its seven SADCC neighbours: more than 2.4 million tonnes of this trade being South African, while 1.6 million tonnes were goods sold to South Africa. The other 2 million tonnes represented overseas SADCC imports/exports.(25) Despite the intention behind the SADCC of decreasing dependence on South African trade and infrastructure, there has been an increase - the 1985/86 figures revealing that of the SADCC's total export/import of 14.95 million tonnes, some 12.5 million tonnes (85 percent) was routed through South Africa. An Economist Intelligence Unit study revealed that all SADCC members, with the exception of Tanzania, have South African trade links: each trade more with South Africa than with all their SADCC partners combined. Total SADCC business with South Africa, then some US$ 2 billion, was seven times higher than intra-SADCC trade.(26)

Should comprehensive international sanctions achieve their sought after goal of sealing South Africa's borders, several regional states would be in immediate difficulty. Swaziland would have to re-route her import/exports through the already heavily congested, unreliable and sporadically disrupted Mozambique transport system. Lesotho is completely surrounded by South African territory and short of an impractical airbridge there is no other way of securing alternative routes. Both Zimbabwe and Zambia could intensify their use of alternative routes: Zimbabwe could concentrate on the Mozambican ports of Nacala and Beira and Zambia could try to increase tonnage carried on the Tanzam rail link to Dar-es-Salaam.

Rail traffic, harbour tonnages and air cargo between South Africa and Southern Africa

1984/85 ★

	Rail Traffic Tonnages		Harbour Traffic Tonnages*		Air Cargo‡
	Imports	Exports	Imports	Exports	(kg)
Botswana	409 059	27 874	48 974	184	220 147
Lesotho	69 233	-	38 994	-	86 378
Malawi	8 283	24 391	5 851	19 788	2 852 972
Mozambique	849 726	805 091	-	-	137 757
Swaziland	56 242	821 898	36 793	775 019	167 988
Zaire	115 504	278 936	33 703	277 182	1 937
Zambia	390 203	122 366	52 419	108 805	505 326
Zimbabwe	1 175 098	797 281	444 752	96 616	2 165 442

★This is the last year for which official statistics have been published; these statistics have been classified since the imposition of sanctions

*Traffic handled at South African harbours

‡Cargo handled by South African Airways together with its pool partners

Source: "Southern Africa Facts Sheet", No 91, January 1987.

The on-going civil war between the Marxist Mozambqiue state and the pro-Western RENAMO movement, however, has severely damaged most of Mozambique's rail and harbour infrastructure, severely hindering its capacity to handle even the comparatively small proportion of Zimbabwean export/import trade that it now does: the Tanzam railroad, despite having been built as a showpiece, is chronically inefficient, with between half and two-thirds of its locomotives disabled at any given time. Already stretched in its handling of just under half of Zambia's trade, it is unlikely that it could cope with any more. The Angolan civil war, similarly between a Marxist-Leninist one-party state and a pro-Western liberation movement, UNITA, has also sealed off the use of the Atlantic Lobito and Benguela harbours, further depriving Zambia and Zimbabwe - as well as Botswana and Zaire - of import/export access.

The extent of South African involvement in the transport infrastructure can be gathered from the fact that during one average month in 1985 alone, there were unilaterally 2,080 South African Transport Service (SATS) railway trucks in Zaire and Zambia: another 2,453 SATS trucks were in Zimbabwe and Botswana while there were 918 Zimbabwean rail trucks on South African lines: a further 1,411 trucks were in Mozambique while 13 Mozambique railways units were on SATS lines. (27)

The sheer hypocracy of frontline statesmen such as Zimbabwe's Robert Mugabe in publically demanding comprehensive sanctions, while privately being party to trade and transport deals, is becoming increasingly evident. Even as Prime Minister Mugabe strongly criticised Mrs Thatcher's anti-sanctions stance at the 1987 Vancouver Commonwealth conference, for example, his government signed an assistance pact with South African transport authorities.(28)

Employment in South Africa

There are some 370,000 non-South African blacks from neighbouring states legally employed within the South African economy.(29) The major countries of origin of these workers being Lesotho, Mozambique, Malawi, Botswana and Swaziland.

REGISTERED FOREIGN WORKERS IN SOUTH AFRICA

Country	Male	Female	Total
Angola	19	3	22
Botswana	26865	1379	28244
Lesotho	134497	3696	138193
Malawi	30749	662	31411
Mozambique	73146	40	73186
Swaziland	20302	1612	21914
Zambia	2410	11	2421
Zimbabwe	7273	31	7304
Other	74747	683	75430
Total	370008	8117	378125

Source: 'Southern African Facts Sheet', No 19, January 1987

Some eighty percent of these contract workers are employed by the South African mining industry. Approximately half of their total earnings, calculated in 1984 as some R400 million, is remitted annually - providing several neighbouring states with a sizeable portion of their national income. In Lesotho, for example, more than fifty percent of the gross national product is derived from remitted earnings of Lesotho migrant workers: of the country's 200,000 workforce, more than 140,000 work in South Africa. Bearing in mind the black African extended family concept, it has been estimated that some two million non-South African black women and children, in addition to their legally employed menfolk, are dependent on the South African economy.

In addition to those legally employed in South Africa, there are an estimated one million other non-South African blacks illegally employed in the country. These workers similarly remit earnings and support families across the region. Comprehensive sanctions would hit both these groups of workers very hard indeed. Even the passionately pro-sanctions United Kingdom-based Catholic Institute for International Relations, while disputing the number involved - arguing somewhat self-defeatingly that **only** 600,000 SADCC nationals work in South Africa - concedes that their wage remittances are "nonetheless critical to the incomes of many SADCC households".(30)

This study of the effects of punitive sanctions upon Southern Africa as a whole has touched primarily on trade, transport and regional black employment. The South African involvement in the region is a multi-facetted one, touching virtually every aspect of day-to-day economic life. The cumulative total of long-term South African financial credit guarantees, for example, to Southern African countries is in excess of R350 million - short term credit extended to black African states comes to more than R250 million annually.(31) In the words of the London 'Financial Times'

"Indeed, in just about every sphere of economic activity - electricity supply, bank credit, tourism, air transport, essential imports especially petrol, but also food grains, fertiliser, and heavy capital equipment - there is a high degree of South African participation or even control. Scope for 'de-linking'... is limited" (32)

The dangers to the region of attempting to impose a serious sanctions/disinvestment package on South Africa were also summed up:

"If it were possible to envisage a short, sharp economic blitz to force political change on Pretoria - Harold Wilson's weeks rather than months - then the damage suffered by the frontline states might be contained to manageable levels. But a prolonged campaign lasting more than five years could have disastrous effects on several countries already classified as among the world's less developed economies - especially if Pretoria were to retaliate vigorously" (33)

Chapter Four
BLACK SOUTH AFRICANS REJECT SANCTIONS

1 IN THEIR OWN WORDS

One of the ironies of the persistent calls by Western leaders, churches and organisations for economic sanctions against, and disinvestment from, South Africa is that they have unmistakably racist overtones. What is in effect happening is that overwhelmingly white institutions, groupings and individuals, themselves economically and socially comfortable, are urging the destruction of black South African jobs. In a clear parody of apartheid at its worst, these white groups and people are turning to the black South African and saying 'we know what is in your best interests - and it is our view that you should lose your job, and through that your house; your family may well suffer and go hungry but that is also in your best interests...'. And if the black South African should demur in any way, these white North Americans and Western Europeans challenge his or her legitimacy in some racist parody of Marxist 'false consciousness'.

There are an increasing number of black South Africans who are willing to publically contradict those self-perceived spokesmen for black South Africans. By far the most prominent is Chief Mangosuthu Buthelezi, Chief Minister of KwaZulu, president of the Inkatha black nationalist movement and chairman of the South African Black Alliance. This organisation comprises, in addition to Inkatha, the Indian Reform Party under Y S Chinsamy, and the Linkoanketla Party, made up largely from the South Sotho people led by Chief Kenneth Mopeli, and has an estimated eight million black and Indian supporters.(1)

Chief Buthelezi has condemned sanctions and disinvestment from every conceivable platform, through newspapers, magazines, key-note speeches at political rallies, meetings with Western political leaders, testimony to the House of Commons and at trade union events.

The depth of Mangosuthu Buthelezi's objection to economic sanctions is very clear:

"I oppose disinvestment and sanctions as vehemently as I oppose the South African government"   (2)

Chief Buthelezi's criticisms have been all encompassing. He has been particularly critical of claims that black South Africans support sanctions:

"I would challenge anyone who said that black people wanted sanctions to go to Johannesburg, to go to Cape Town...Durban and other cities, and see how many hundreds of black people are queueing up for jobs...they are voting with their feet for more investment and for jobs" (3)

Referring to the Inkatha nationalist movement, an organisation with 1.3 million card-carrying black members:

"It is in Soweto that I hold...my annual rallies...up to 40,000 fill a soccer stadium to express their solidarity with Inkatha and encourage its leadership to continue on course...No year passes without my putting the disinvestment question before Inkatha's annual general conference. This body of 3,000-4,000 representatives - elected by the people at local branch and regional level - every year unanimously rejects disinvestment...No year passes when I do not address mass meetings in different parts of the country - and every year thousands of ordinary South Africans roar their disapproval of disinvestment as a strategy" (4)

Despite Chief Buthelezi's powerbase being in KawZulu/Natal, the Inkatha movement enjoys support throughout the black community. A study conducted in 1977 by the Arnold Bergstrasse Institute of Freiburg University in West Germany, indicated that 40 percent of Inkatha supporters in Soweto, for example, were not Zulus.(5)

Chief Buthelezi was also present at the launch, on May Day 1986, of the United Workers Union of South Africa, (UWUSA). The result of large scale disatisfaction with existing trade unions, and their increased role in radical politics at the expense of genuine worker interests, UWUSA was launched at a rally attended by 70 - 80,000 black South Africans. Buthelezi repeatedly asked the crowd for their feelings on sanctions:

"...they roared their disapproval while waving placards which condemned Bishop Desmond Tutu for supporting the type of action which would deprive them of employment and food (6)

In testimony to the British House of Commons Foreign Affairs Committee in 1986, Chief Buthelezi was critical of the effect sanctions would have on the economic and political enfranchisement of black South Africans:

"Whereas in the past the government did not allow blacks to perform certain jobs...economic reality has caused it to fall away to the extent that participation by blacks in the trade union movement has come about and has increased buying power, and mobility of blacks in the political field. If this was allowed to happen more and more it will not be difficult to extend it to political interdependence. That is why I say we need massive and sustained economic growth in South Africa for the purpose of change; that is why I say sanctions cannot solve the problem for us" (7)

The inherent contradictions of wanting to destroy an economy in order to bring well-being to those dependent on that economy for life itself were also pointed out by Chief Buthelezi:

"For liberation to have a meaning for the ordinary people, you must improve the quality of their life. You cannot have a situation where you destroy the economy of the country, because whoever runs the country will have problems" (8)

This was a point also raised by Dr Oscar Dhlomo, secretary general of Inkatha and KwaZulu Minister of Education and Culture, in his testimony to the British Foreign Affairs Committee in 1986:

"One wrong thing the West could do would be to fail to differentiate between apartheid as an evil system and South Africa as a country inhabited by an oppressed black majority...sanctions do not make that distinction. So if we were going to claim that you were assisting the victims of apartheid by imposing sanctions on South Africa you would be acting as somebody who bombs the cells in order to free the prisoners" (9)

Dr Dhlomo went on to state that sanctions assume:

"...that if South Africa is strangled economically then all of a sudden South Africa would change course and become a democracy and include the excluded majority. Now we are not sure, and is it fair to gamble with the lives of millions and millions of people when you are not even sure that the effect of sanctions is what we speculate it will be?" (10)

The dangers of the severe economic dislocation that would follow any coherent sanctions programme have been clearly outlined by Percy Qoboza.

A long-standing black opponent of apartheid, Qoboza was the former editor of the WORLD newspaper and is now associate editor of CITY PRESS. The WORLD was deemed a dangerously radical newspaper and was banned, together with the range of Black Consciousness publications and organisations, in October 1977. Because of his radically anti-apartheid stance Percy Qoboza was detained without trial for almost five months in the late 1970s. Speaking to the South African-British Trade Association in June 1985 Qoboza, in condemning sanctions and disinvestment, argued that there was no clear support for either amongst black South Africans. The struggle for political power by blacks is not in itself enough - to make life meaningful, economic resources are also needed. This would not arise out of the economic chaos that would result from disinvestment:

"If you want a complete transformation of this society, the easiest thing to do is get everybody packing up their bags, taking their money out of the country and resisting all forms of investment in the country. But of course the moment you do that you create economic chaos. And that is a sure guarantee for full-scale bloody racial confrontation which would unleash a bloodbath such as we have never seen. Therefore, this is clearly not consistent with my own belief that we must seek a peaceful transformation of society" (11)

(NOTE: At the time of going to press news was received in London of the death of Mr Qoboza - on his 50th birthday. His obituary was given wide coverage by the world's press)

The role played by foreign capital in bringing pressure to bear on the South African government was one reason cited by internationally-recognised anti-apartheid activist, Steve Biko, for his opposition to disinvestment. A radical student leader, and president of the Black Peoples Convention (BPC), Steve Biko was the political force behind the 'Black Consciousness' movement that swept South Africa throughout the mid-and-late 1970s. He was detained and charged under security legislation on numerous occasions, spending 101 days in detention under section 6 of the Terrorism Act in 1976. Detained again in August 1977, he died in police custody one month later. Biko's analysis of the role of foreign investment was clear:

"We are of the belief that if we are to move towards a peaceful solution our efforts must be coupled with suppport from other people...and we see this whole foreign investments question as a possible vehicle for generating pressure to sympathise with our point of view so that South Africa can listen, not only to us but also to other people"(12)

Steve Biko also recognised the practical assistance provided by foreign investment in South African commerce and industry:

"We wanted foreign investors to help in the build-up of the humanity of the blacks, to give them opportunity for training in technical sphere, to recognise to some extent trade union work within the firms, in a sense to encourage humanity amongst blacks who are employed by them, negating the whole effect of apartheid on blacks in this country" (13)

Bearing in mind Steve Biko's key role in the struggle for black liberation in South Africa, his having been literally at the forefront of the conflict against apartheid, surely his views in support of constructive investment count for more than the average white, politically-motivated British, Western European or American advocate of disinvestment and sanctions.

Lucy Mvubelo is another prominent black anti-apartheid activist who rejects sanctions and disinvestment. A trade union worker and anti-apartheid activist for more than forty years, and general secretary of the Clothing Workers of South Africa for thirty of them, Mrs Mvubelo has a lifetime's experience of fighting for black union and political rights. A former vice-president of the now defunct Trade Union Council of South Africa, which represented some 400,000 workers in 56 unions, she was also elected Life President of the Business and Professional Women's Society in 1973, she was awarded an honorary doctorate in social science by Rhodes University and was also the first black woman to serve on the National Manpower Commission, the NMC being the institution responsible for totally reforming South Africa's labour laws. Mrs Mvubelo has seen the effects of economic interaction with overseas capital:

"Foreign investment has created jobs for thousands of African workers who would otherwise be unemployed. Thanks to the policies of foreign firms operating here, black workers have gained significant wage increases, often larger than the increases gained by black workers in South African companies."

"By insisting on the withdrawal of foreign companies - even of only American firms - disinvestment advocates are asking a substantial number of blacks to sacrifice their jobs, to sacrifice their only realistic means of attaining wider opportunities and higher living standards" (14)

Having heard all the arguments for and against external economic pressures, Mrs Mvubelo remains unconvinced.

While not agreeing about much else, both Chief Lennox Sebe, president of the Ciskei national state within South Africa and Chief George Mantanzima, the recently deposed prime minister of the Transkei, reject sanctions as indisputably hostile to black South African interests.

Speaking in September 1986 President Sebe, reiterating his hatred of the "abhorrent practice" of apartheid, also attacked the international remedy of economic measures aimed at crippling the South African economy:

"We are an intra-dependent society, and while there are defined boundaries for South African and its independent states, there are so many issues that can only effectively be dealt with on a community basis. We have never advocated economic suicide and would appeal to those in positions of power throughout the world to think again and abandon their sanctions campaign and prevent the bringing about of economic collapse leading to further suffering, hardship, disorder and violence" (15)

Chief Matanzima termed pro-sanctions church leaders such as Desmond Tutu, "prophets of doom" unconcerned about the real situation of South African blacks. (16)

Another elected black South African leader, Dr Cedric Phatudi - until his recent death the Chief Minister of the self-governing state of Lebowa also strenuously opposed sanctions and disinvestment. Appearing before the British Foreign Affairs Committee, Dr Phatudi also challenged the idea that black South Africans support sanctions:

"...a large majority of blacks in Southern Africa are strenuously opposed to punitive sanctions imposed on South Africa" (17)

He attacked the whole concept of sanctions as "a futile exercise by all standards" which "have never succeeded anywhere" and which would inevitably hurt black South Africans:

"Disinvestment is supposed to help the blacks. This is a serious error. Disinvestment kills the blacks. How can you help blacks by killing them?" (18)

Dr Phatudi was particularly concerned at the damage that sanctions and disinvestment would have on the South African reform process:

"Ironically, sanctions appear to have made our Government slow down its own reform programme. It has also been said that major reform will in all likelihood remain unattended to while the Government focuses on two priorities: solidifying its position through elections, and the various dimensions of a counter-sanctions programme in place"

"...disinvestment will delay the termination of apartheid and in the process bring suffering to those it is intended to help" (19)

The emergence of a strong black entrepreneurial class within South Africa has been a very welcome development. Their voice effectively is the 'National African Federated Chamber of Commerce, (NAFCOC). NAFCOC is a national organisation with eighteen affiliated regional chambers throughout South Africa, each regional chamber having affiliated local chambers of commerce. NAFCOC's many projects include the African Bank, the Aribrokers insurance company, Blackchain supermarkets, an Entrepreneurship Training Programme, an Industrial Counselling Committee, construction companies, and a publishing house. A long standing opponent of apartheid, perceiving it, in the words of NAFCOC president Sam Motsuenyane, as "a socialist set-up" legislating against free enterprise, the organisation has campaigned long and hard against apartheid and in favour of free enterprise. The National African Federated Chambers of Commerce has also been highly critical of the apartheid regime. At NAFCOC's 21st annual conference in 1985 resolutions passed included the following:
-   The dismantling of apartheid
-   Freeing Nelson Mandela and all political prisoners
-   Unbanning both the African National Congress and Pan Africanist Congress
-   Granting full citizenship rights to all South Africans
-   The Scrapping of all discriminatory legislation
-   The Abolition of all residential and business segregation

(20)

NAFCOC has also held meetings in Lusaka with the African National Congress. Against this track record of opposition to apartheid, this exclusively black South African organisation strongly opposes the concept of sanctions and disinvestment. Mr P G Gumede, vice-president of NAFCOC and president of the Inyanda Chamber of Commerce believes that disinvestment would be disastrous for all South Africans. He said that black South Africans found it difficult to believe that economic measures of that sort could be to their benefit. His experience was that foreign companies had pioneered desirable labour reforms and in the event of any retrenchment due to sanctions, blacks would be the first to suffer. Opposition to punitive economic measures against South Africa was shared by all South Africans, black or white:

"If there is anything which should unite South Africans across the colour line it is the issue of sanctions" (21)

Several elected local government leaders have also made their opposition to sanctions clear. Amongst them is the former mayor of Soweto, David Thebehali:

"Mr Average Soweto wants a job, education, a house, a good environment...Sanctions and disinvestment can only harm the people they (disinvestment activists) want to help" (22)

Returning from a visit to Canada timed to coincide with the 1987 Commonwealth Conference, Esau Mahlatsi, the mayor of the black town of Sebokeng, was highly critical of sanctions. The imposition of sanctions against South Africa had been a "most unwise" policy move by Western nations he said. In doing so he also reaffirmed his opposition to apartheid:

"Disagreeing with sanctions doesn't mean that I agree with apartheid...Apartheid in South Africa is on the way out and there is already a visible improvement in our living conditions" (23)

Similar views against sanctions can be heard from every section of black South African society. James Ngcoya, president of the Southern African Bus and Taxi Association has declared:

"Changes in our country today need active constructive support it does not need the penalty of sanctions" (24)

As part of the reform process within South Africa both the Indian and Coloured communities were enfranchised into what is now the Tricameral Parliament of South Africa. Both communities elected legislators to their respective chambers. These Coloured and Indian parliamentarians have also been openly hostile to the idea of immediate punitive sanctions. The House of Representatives, the Coloured chamber, for example, called for a five year moratorium on disinvestment. Peter Hendrickse, son of the Labour Party leader who is one of the two Coloured members of the Cabinet, introduced the motion in the House because:

50

"...the government has said it is sincere about reform. Give us a chance, one could say a last chance, to bring about change peacefully"

(25)

Pat Poovalingam, an Indian Member of the South African Parliament, couched his rejection of sanctions in terms of the cost to those South Africans they were misguidedly intended to help:

"Those in the United States and elsewhere who would impose economic sanctions against South Africa would strap the victim as well as the perpetrator of the crime to the electric chair...There are those who argue, rather glibly, that it is inevitable that suffering will be imposed on black and brown South Africans by economic sanctions: that this is a price that has to be paid. Interestingly most of those who purvey this argument are living outside South Africa"

Chapter Five

BLACK SOUTH AFRICAN OPINION POLLS ON SANCTIONS AND DISINVESTMENT

Introduction

There can be no doubt that a key element in the debate surrounding punitive economic measures against South Africa is whether black South Africans actually support such measures. There have been several attempts to ascertain black views on the issue through social surveys and opinion polls.

The past three years have seen twelve such surveys. While there has been a certain level of confusion surrounding one or two conclusions, the general indication has been that a large majority of black South Africans are not in favour of sanctions/disinvestment.

1 THE 1984 SCHLEMMER REPORT

The first ever key survey of black worker opinion was the June-August 1984 poll by Professor Lawrence Schlemmer, then a member of the University of Natal's Centre for Applied Social Sciences. A former president of the South African Institute of Race Relations, and heavily linked to Indicator SA, a Natal University-backed research and publishing project, Professor Schlemmer is one of South Africa's foremost political scientists and an eminent sociologist. This survey involved a representative sample of 551 black factory workers, aged from 16 to 50 plus years of age, in seven major industrial regions throughout the country. Conducted by skilled black field-workers away from the work place, the disinvestment issue was discussed in six different questions in interviews averaging some 110 minutes each. Some 65% were classified lower semi-skilled and 35% higher semi-skilled and skilled. The results recorded a 75 percent rejection of punitive economic measures among black workers, support for disinvestment dropping to as little as nine percent in one question.

There have been several attempts to discredit this particular poll and its devasting implications for those advocating sanctions. One of the most common arguments used is the supposed impossibility of black South Africans speaking out honestly on a controversial issue such as sanctions/disinvestment. A typical attack is that carried in 'The Roots of Crisis in Southern Africa' by American Oxfam:

"Supporters of continued U.S. investment in South Africa claim most black South Africans support it. However, expressing opposition to foreign investment is a crime punishable by a minimum of five years in jail and a maximum of the death penalty. This renders questionable the outcome of the 1984 Schlemmer poll of 551 workers employed in U.S. companies. The survey, paid for in part by the Reagan administration, claimed 75 percent of those polled opposed divestment. The fact that 25 percent dared to speak in favor, despite heavy punishment if their identities were revealed, suggests instead strong support for divestment" (1)

What the Oxfam piece conveniently ignores is that in the same poll, the same black South Africans were confident enough of their interviewers impartiality to also express a high degree of support for the outlawed African National Congress - support which could very well result in prosecution under South African law.

In August 1986 Professor Schlemmer published a comparison of ten of the opinion polls/social surveys dating from June 1984 to July 1986. His conclusion was that:

"In overview, then, the full range of surveys leads me to the conclusion that at this stage only a minority of blacks in major metropolitan areas would support total disinvestment or economic boycotts"(2)

In the two surveys carried out by Professor Schlemmer (June-August 1984 and November 1986) an average of 80 percent of the blacks interviewed rejected disinvestment.

Surveys conducted by the South African Human Sciences Research Council (HSRC) (July 1984, February 1985 and May 1985) indicated that an average of seventy-four percent of blacks polled rejected the concept of an overseas economic boycott of South Africa.(3) A further HSRC poll taken in September 1986 among 1,459 black adults and 372 black youths showed a 59.4 percent rejection of punitive economic measures against South Africa: 29.6% were in favour and 11 percent had no opinion.

2 THE LONDON 'SUNDAY TIMES' POLL

In August 1986, the London 'Sunday Times' published the results of a poll they had commissioned to test black South African feelings towards sanctions.(4) Carried out for the 'Sunday Times' by

Market and Opinion Research International (Mori) and the South African company Markinor, the results overturned the pro-sanctions findings of the 1985 'Sunday Times' poll. A representative sample of 615 black South Africans - this time including both urban **and** rural areas indicated that more blacks opposed economic sanctions against their country than supported them. Thirty-two percent opposed sanctions while twenty-nine were in favour of them. The rest of those polled had either no opinion on the issue or had never heard of sanctions. 44 percent of blacks thought they would personally suffer as the result of the imposition of punitive economic sanctions.

These findings corrected the 1985 poll which was patently unrepresentative in its concentration on a black urban sample.

3   THE COMMUNITY AGENCY FOR SOCIAL ENQUIRY/IRB SURVEYS

Two polls which indicated black South African support for sanctions - surveys conducted in 1985 and 1987 by Mark Orkin of the Community Agency for Social Enquiry/Institute for Black Research - have been heavily criticised for their methodology. Although lauded as conclusive proof of black support for sanctions, if the results are interpreted according to the same criteria as the Schlemmer survey, they are similar is theme. In Orkin's 1985 survey, 800 black South Africans in ten major metropolitan areas were polled. The 1987 poll included a large proportion of rural black South Africans. His questions in both polls have been heavily criticised for being unscientific and misleading. Orkin's disinvestment question is incredibly long, more than 225 words, and links the three options listed with political parties and politicians. The ANC/PAC/UDF and certain unions, for instance, are cited as opposing investment because it 'only help(s) to keep apartheid alive and exploit Blacks': Archbishop Tutu is mentioned as a supporter of conditional investment and Buthelezi is lumped together with the government, other homeland leaders and Harry Oppenheimer as sharing a stance favourable to investment. The question for those opposing sanctions read: "This view is supported by P W Botha, and the Nationalist government, by the PFP, by businessmen like Harry Oppenheimer and by homeland leaders like Chief Buthelezi".

The subjective phrasing of the Orkin survey has been challenged by others active in the field of sanctions opinion testing. Professor Schlemmer claimed that the sanctions question's options were confusingly linked to political leadership:

"I am surprised that as many as 26 percent of people oppose sanctions given that to do so would be to associate with the government. That this has been done biases the response against rejection of sanctions

This is not comparable with other surveys and the respondent is faced with the critical dilemma to support sanctions or his political leadership" (5)

If analysed correctly, however, Orkin's results correlate with Professor Schlemmer's:

	Orkin	Schlemmer
Pro-Investment	26	75
Conditionally pro-investment	49	
Anti-investment	24	25
Don't know	1	-

(6)

The August/September 1987 Orkin poll revealed much the same result. Fifty-two percent polled were conditionally pro-investment and 14 percent totally opposed to sanctions. Orkin posed a new question in the latest poll - whether respondents were prepared to continue supporting sanctions if these resulted in job losses for blacks. This question produced some very interesting results. Sixty percent of black South Africans polled rejected sanctions if they involved job losses. Twenty-six percent were willing to accept some, but not many, blacks unemployed as a result of sanctions. Only fourteen percent stood by the sanctions position whatever the unemployment costs.(6) Nonetheless, Orkin claimed that:

"Taken together, the results illuminate the policy decisions on sanctions of the unions, the churches and popular political tendencies...They are calling for sanctions to be comprehensive rather than voluntary, in the hope that this way sanctions will achieve the greatest possible impact, while causing unavoidable economic hardship for the shortest possible time" (7)

For Orkin to cite support for comprehensive sanctions, guaranteed to cause massive unemployment, while the results of his poll indicate a 60 percent rejection of any punitive economic measures leading to job losses, indicates the desperate level to which some social scientists will sink in order to claim black South African support for sanctions.

4 THE APRIL 1987 SURVEY

In April 1987, the South African Bureau for Information commissioned a private research company to test black, Coloured and Indian opinion on the sanctions/disinvestment issue. A nation-wide sample of 4,500 metropolitan and rural blacks, 500 Coloureds and 500 Indians was examined.

The response to questions raised in the poll was very interesting. The replies to the question: "There are groups of people in South Africa and overseas who try to encourage banks and companies not to invest in South Africa. Do you think this is a good thing, neither good nor bad, a bad thing or do you not know?":

RESPONSE	Percentage of Respondents		
	Black	Coloured	Indian
A good thing	12.9	13.8	7.2
Neither good nor bad	5.2	16.4	3.0
A bad thing	78.7	69.0	89.2
Don't know	3.2	0.8	0.6

The main reasons cited as motivation for deeming punitive economic measures to be "a bad thing" were unemployment, a drop in living standards, disinvestment from South Africa and a failing economy.

In results of answers to the question: "There are groups of people who try to prevent South African goods and products from being sold in countries overseas. Do you think this is a good thing, neither good nor bad, a bad thing or do you not know?":

RESPONSE	Percentage of Respondents		
	Black	Coloured	Indian
A good thing	15.4	17.2	7.0
Neither good nor bad	6.0	12.4	2.8
A bad thing	75.3	69.8	90.2
Don't know	3.4	0.6	--

Reasons again cited for having responded negatively were unemployment, starvation and poverty, black suffering, the handicap on job creation, price rises, an increase in crime and a drop in the standard of living.

CONCLUSION
The results of by far the majority of surveys of black South African opinion on the disinvestment/sanctions issue overwhelmingly show a rejection of punitive economic measures. Professor Schlemmer's August 1986 conclusions in his survey of surveys, Mark Orkin's 1987 CASE/IBR survey notwithstanding, hold true:

At this stage it can still be said that no survey has proved that a majority of blacks are willing to endorse punitive economic sanctions which would reduce the capacity of the economy to create jobs and welfare''

(8)

Chapter Six
ANTI-APARTHEID
AND ANTI-SANCTIONS

In addition to black South Africans at the forefront of the anti-apartheid struggle who perceive punitive economic measures as hindering the chances of black economic and political liberation, there are also a large number of white South Africans, equally committed to the total destruction of apartheid, who similarly see the dangers inherent in the imposition of sanctions and disinvestment. One cannot ignore the views of such long-standing, committed anti-apartheid activists as Helen Suzman and Alan Paton.

There has always been considerable political opposition to the government and the policies of apartheid within South Africa. This has taken the form of pro-Marxist resistance politics as represented by the African National Congress/South African Communist Party Alliance; democratic, pro-Western/free market values as represented by Chief Mangosuthu Buthelezi and of the liberal/left parliamentary and business opposition to apartheid, personified by Helen Suzman and industrialists such as Harry Oppenheimer. The views of this latter grouping of South Africans in their opposition to sanctions is just as relevant to the sanctions debate as those of their black, Coloured and Indian compatriots - and in most instances, echoes their concerns and feelings on the issue. It is, after all, South Africans - white and black - who are more in tune with the reality of South Africa today, with what must be done to totally eradicate apartheid from South African society, and who are the best judges of what stands to encourage or endanger this process.

Until the May 6 1987 election for the white house of the South African Tricameral Parliament, the Progressive Federal Party (PFP), was the official opposition to President P W Botha's Nationalist government. Having lost seven seats in the May election, it was displaced by the hardline, pro-apartheid Conservative Party, which then weighed in with 22 parliamentary seats to the PFP's seventeen. The Progressive Federal Party has long been the most prominent and organised liberal opposition to apartheid. The party, under the leadership of Dr Frederick Van Zyl Slabbert, campaigned fiercely against the new constitution as presented by then prime minister Botha in 1983. Perhaps the PFP's most noted leader and parliamentarian is Mrs Helen Suzman. For thirteen years her party's only parliamentary representative and vociferous apartheid antagonist she has opposed the concept of punitive economic measures for two decades. There was a distinct role for pressurising the South African government:

"The West should raise its voice long and hard against apartheid in general and in particular against any outrageous actions by the South African government...

The South African government is more sensitive than one thinks. It does not enjoy being a pariah. It would like to be welcomed back into the Western community of nations. But not at any cost. Rather you should aim at attainable objectives than adopt measures that could reduce the country to economic chaos, with totally unpredictable consequences" (1)

Mrs Suzman views the introduction of sanctions and disinvestment as self-defeating and contradictory.

"Self-defeating because it blunts the one weapon that blacks are able to use to insist that their demands be accomodated - the power to withdraw skilled labour" (2)

Dealing with the view that black South Africans support sanctions and are willing to endure the drastic consequences of such economic measures Mrs Suzman is critical:

"I am at the receiving end of many requests from recent job losers for assistance in obtaining jobs, and I say that blacks who don't care are those whose jobs are not endangered or who have never had a job to lose" (3)

These were views shared with the former leader of the Progressive Federal Party, Dr Van Zyl Slabbert. An Afrikaner and a former academic turned politician, Dr Slabbert has long been a critic of the Nationalist government and apartheid. His very public resignation from both the South African Parliament and the leadership of the PFP was - in part - due to the slowing down of the government's reform process. He now heads a think tank dedicated to bringing blacks and whites politically and socially closer together, drawing strong government criticism for having helped organise the much publicised meeting between the ANC and various white South Africans in Dakar, Senegal in 1987.

Dr Slabbert's criticism of the whole concept of sanctions is multifacetted, covering all the points raised by the pro-sanctions lobby. Sanctions will not force the government's hand: "the evidence is overwhelmingly to the contrary...the government tends to become more obdurate". He is particularly critical of the idea that black South Africans cannot suffer any more than they are at the moment and therefore any punitive economic measures will weaken the government, bringing about the eventual downfall of the state. What is ignored is that things could get considerably worse without any improvement politically at all - and that through this the government could conceivably become stronger and more coercive. Dr Slabbert also touched on the alternatives that exist to sanctions:

"If you can assist blacks in education that is a government-to-government pressure; it is also private-enterprise-to-private-enterprise pressure. The pressures that come about of, say, multinationals improving the quality of life and the working conditions of people there are a form of indirect pressure that builds up inside that situation. Diplomatic pressure, no doubt, can be brought about in the sense that you can say that if certain things do not happen you will withdraw or call back your respresentative" (4)

A further prominent white critic of apartheid and the concept of sanctions is Alan Paton. The former national president of the multiracial Liberal Party, which disbanded itself in 1968 rather than fall in line with then apartheid legislation confining its membership to one racial grouping, and author of the famous 'Cry the Beloved Country' Alan Paton is passionately opposed to disinvestment:

"There is only one firm statement that I can make on disinvestment that I will have nothing to do with it. I will not, by any written or spoken word, give it any support whatsoever.

Why am I totally opposed to disinvestment? It is primarily for a moral reason. It is my firm belief that those who will pay most grievously for disinvestment will be the black workers of South Africa...

I am also told that I am ignoring the view of those black South Africans who support disinvestment. Most of these black South Africans will not be the ones to suffer hunger and thirst. Many of them are sophisticated, highly educated, safely placed...There is an often-heard declaration: 'We do not mind suffering. We are used to suffering'. But this again is often the declaration of those who will suffer least"(5)

Paton also criticises advocates of disinvestment for their short-sightedness. He asks for how long people will have to suffer before the attainment of the desired effect: "A month? Two months? A year? Five or ten years perhaps?":

"No one can confidently answer that question though one can say at once that disinvestment will take time to bite deep. South Africa's business community will muster every resource to save the economy from destruction" (6)

He also echoes the views of black trade union activists such as Lucy Mvubelo in speculating as to some of the true motivations behind the advocacy of sanctions and disinvestment:

"I have no doubt that some supporters of disinvestment hope that it will not only cause such severe damage to the economy, but will also increase endemic unrest to such an extent that armed revolution will take place, and that the present government will be overthrown by force of arms" (7)

Harry Oppenheimer has been a persistent thorn in the side of the South African government for several decades. A former chairman of the giant Anglo-American and De Beers corporations, he spent several years in parliament as a United Party representative before helping to form the Progressive Party - now the Progressive Federal Party. Mr Oppenheimer has seen, and chronicled, noticeable changes within both South African politics and society over the past ten years - changes for the better for black South Africans. These include the recognition of black trade unions; rapid rises in black wages; increased powers of local self-government; the scrapping of the policy of job reservation; the review of influx control; and the acceptance of urban black populations, to name but a few. He speaks for the vast majority of people, black and white, South African or North American when he states that South Africa is heading towards a post-apartheid situation:

"Change in South Africa is inevitable and is accepted as inevitable as well as desirable by the vast majority of the population. The only question is how it should be brought about. Economic growth leads to peaceful change; economic stagnation to violent change. Those inside and outside South Africa, who genuinely want to see peaceful change for the better should do all they can to facilitate economic growth and prosperity and to eliminate unemployment. And here a high level of foreign investment is a factor of vital importance"(8)

The damage that would be caused by an effective disinvestment or sanctions campaign is clear:

"If the necessary level of investment and the skills associated with it are not made available, industrial growth will decline, racial conflict will sharpen, the 'laager' mentality among whites will become stronger, real earnings will stagnate and eventually fall, unemployment will increase...This may not be what the disinvestment lobby aims at. But nevertheless it is the logical outcome of the policy they pursue. And if they were to succeed...they would have done more to implement the apartheid policy than all the South African Government could manage by its influx control and pass laws"   (9)

Harry Oppenheimer has warned that both apartheid and sanctions would have the same effect:

"The rigid application of the apartheid policy also would have led to misery, despair and eventual revolution in South Africa and that is why it is now being abandoned. Effective economic sanctions would lead to the same end by a different route."   (10)

The 1985-86 annual report of the Anglo-American Corporation can be seen as being representative of most business, commercial and industrial interests, in its warning of the potentially grave consequences of sanctions and disinvestment:

"We must hope that western nations, in particular, will not allow themselves to be pressured into adopting punitive measures which would undermine both the transitional phase and the success of the post-apartheid society. The West as much as South Africa needs to take decisions that are soundly informed by a strategic vision of their long-term consequences. Any action taken now, primarily as an emotional response to the gravity of the situation here, is bound to be at the expense of freedom and justice in South Africa for if our nascent and democratic institutions are denied a strong economic underpinning they will certainly give way to tyranny."   (11)

It must be realised that, as outlined in an earlier part of this work, commerce and industry in South Africa is inherently hostile to the whole concept of apartheid. Because of its inherently socialistic nature and myriad of restrictions on economic activity, the market and market forces automatically come into conflict with apartheid concepts.

Chapter Seven
THE CHURCH DIMENSION

Various religious organisations and Church leaders have been at the forefront of the clamour for sanctions. These calls have been from international bodies as well as from leading clerics, churches and religious organisations based within South Africa. These calls for sanctions can be challenged from two perspectives. One is the obvious lack of interest in, and unwillingness to accurately ascertain, black South African opinion on the issue of sanctions. A typical example of this doctrinaire attitude is "The Scope for Sanctions: Economic measures Against South Africa", a detailed 102-page pro-sanctions report published by the 'Catholic Institute for International Relations' in Britain.(1)

In the entire 102 pages the crucial question of whether black South Africans support sanctions or disinvestment is dealt with in **nine** lines - reaching the conclusion that because "democratic expression" was denied in South Africa it would be hard to prove that blacks did not endorse economic measures against the government. The publication ignores several reputable anti-sanctions polls, and the repeatedly stated, consistent rejection of sanctions and disinvestment by millions of South Africans as voiced by Chief Buthelezi and Inkatha, elected black political leaders, black trade unionists, and businessmen. This patent disregard for what black South Africans wish is a consistent theme in several Church and other religious calls for economic measures.

The second point concerning the advocacy of sanctions and disinvestment by clerics or church organisations such as the South African Council of Churches (SACC), is that by their very nature they are socially, economically and very often politically isolated from the black people of South Africa, and hence out of touch.

Dr Cedric Phatudi, in his 1986 testimony to the British House of Commons All-Party Foreign Affairs Committee, touched on this point.

"Let us make efforts to kill apartheid and not kill a black man. Yet there are those who advocate measures that will kill a black man instead of apartheid... We note that among the apostles of punitive sanctions on South Africa there are some of the leading clergy in our land"

(2)

The Chief Minister challenged the right of various clerics to demand the imposition of sanctions:

"The clergy do not understand the problem at grassroots level, where people are already starving, deprived, humiliated and injured. The time has really come, in my humble opinion, for the clergy to impose 'fasting' on themselves. Then they will appreciate what hardships the ordinary mass of black people will suffer if punitive sanctions are imposed on South Africa" (3)

When asked during the House of Commons testimony about the pro-sanctions views of Archbishop Desmond Tutu, Dr Phatudi replied that in addition to being the elected leader of Lebowa, he was also the chairman of the Committee of Chief Ministers of the self-governing national states within South Africa. These were KwaZulu with six million people; Lebowa, with four and a half million citizens; GaZankulu, with one and a half million; and both Qwa Qwa and KaNgwane, with one million inhabitants each.

Through this committee he represented the elected leaders of some 14 million black South Africans opposed to sanctions:

"With due respect, Bishop Tutu is head of a church, but I am not sure of whether the church is behind him, but the church alone cannot match the figure I have given you... I am speaking now on behalf of millions of people" (4)

In this critique of the relevance of clerical pronouncements to genuine black economic and political liberation, Dr Phatudi perhaps unwittingly echoed views not dissimilar to those of 'Black Consciousness' leader Steve Biko:

"(B)ureaucratisation and institutionalisation tends to make the Church removed from important priorities and to concentrate on secondary and tertiary functions like structures and finance etc. Because of this, the Church has become very irrelevant and in fact an 'ivory' tower as some people refer to it.

Going hand in hand with the bureaucratisation and institutionalisation of the Church is a special brand of a problem which also makes the Church extremely irrelevant - the concentration of that bureaucracy and institutionalisation in the hands of white people"
(5)

Leading moderate trade unionist, Lucy Mvubelo, shares Biko's reluctance to accept certain church and clerical pressures for sanctions as either salient or in keeping with representative black views on the subject:

Christian churches in America and elsewhere have taken the lead in the international struggle against apartheid. Unfortunately, church leaders are often misguided and often ill-informed, and their statements and activities remain unexamined in light of the actual conditions in South Africa"
(6)

That ordinary black South Africans have objections to being represented by church leaders such as Archbishop Tutu in his calls for sanctions is now becoming a common feature of the debate surrounding sanctions. Mayor Esau Mahlatsi of Sebokeng, an official elected by his black constituents, has challenged Tutu's mandate for such claims:

"Canada has also received Archbishop Desmond Tutu, and they accept him as one of our representatives, but by whom has he been elected?

I don't agree with the Archbishop that sanctions should be imposed and that black people are prepared to suffer for a real democracy"(7)

That such calls for sanctions are starting to backfire on radical proponents such as Tutu can be seen in the case of Elliott Ngwenya, an unemployed black doctor from Guguletu near Cape Town:

"We have been duped by the priests and the politicians... Tutu and Boesak made it sound like the government would fall down as soon as there were disinvestment and sanctions. If that had happened, I would have said sanctions and disinvestment were good. But they failed to change things. All they are bringing is more suffering for us blacks"
(8)

The Church dimension on the sanctions debate is an interesting one - and one which warrants deeper investigation. Despite being economically, socially and politically isolated from the mass of black South Africans - calls for, and pronouncements on sanctions by church leaders such as Desmond Tutu have been held up as representative of black opinion. Archbishop Tutu is the head of the Anglican Church in South Africa.

Black South African religious affiliation may well be an important tool in assessing the degree of black support for sanctions. Desmond Tutu's Anglican Church is a multiracial one which claims just over one million black members, some 5.7 percent of the black South African population.(9) Conceivably therefore Archbishop Tutu could claim to represent his one million black members in his advocacy of sanctions.

Using this litmus test, however, there are several considerably more representative sources for views on sanctions and disinvestment. The largest black Christian organisation, the Reformed Independent Churches Association (RICA), representative of some 864 churches and demoninations, and encompassing more than four million black members is headed by Bishop Isaac Mokoena.(10) Together with the Zionist Christian Church (ZCC), with five million members the largest independent church in Southern Africa, the Reformed Independent Churches Association can be seen as a far more credible representative of black Christian opinion.

Both Bishop Mokoena and Bishop Barnabas Lekganyane - the spiritual leader of the Zionist Christian Church - have strongly and consistently voiced their opposition to sanctions. Both of these senior leaders of black South African Christians would have much more ground in claiming to speak on behalf of black South Africa.

The increasing international focus on, and misguided acceptance of the unrepresentative views of certain church leaders has led to almost unprecendented expressions of concern by traditional leaders in South Africa. King Goodwill Zwelithini ka Bhekuzulu of the Zulus, leader of some seven million black South Africans, speaking in July 1986, made two vital points on the issue. Firstly he warned his people:

"...beware of preachers of the Gospel that will increasingly be seen urging our people to support the politics of desperation, and the politics of violence under the cloak of religion" (11)

Moving on to the abuse of clerical institutions, King Goodwill stated that:

"There have been definite efforts to use mainline Churches as a cover for party political thinking and action. Nowhere is this more demonstrated than it is by the South African Council of Churches" (12)

The above-mentioned South African Council of Churches is, not surprisingly, another strong advocate of sanctions. The views of the SACC are represented overseas as somehow being representative of black opinion in South Africa. One indication, however, of how isolated the South African Council of Churches is from mainstream South Africa can be ascertained from an examination of its finances. In stark contrast to the Reformed Independent Christian Association and the Zionist Christian Church, both of whom are entirely funded by contributions from black members, only 1.2 percent of SACC funding comes from South African sources.(13) Yet it is the South African Council of Churches, as patently unrepresentative as it is, which is cited as proof of support for disinvestment "inside South Africa" by the British 'War on Want' charity/campaigning organisation.(14)

In an interesting turnabout, the Southern African Catholic Bishops' Conference, previously an advocate of economic pressure on the South African government, has had to rethink its policy. In a May 1986 convention, the Catholic Bishops Conference under Archbishop Denis Hurley of Durban, perceived economic measures to be:

"(T)he most effective of non-violent forms of pressure...Economic pressure has been justifiably imposed to end apartheid...such pressure should continue and, if necessary, be intensified"

The reversal of this pro-sanctions stance came in the light of the findings of a commission set up by the Conference to examine the effects of punitive economic measures. The report of the Commission on Economic Pressure found that:

"The whole sanctions issue has consolidated government in its retreat from meaningful, and, indeed, any reform"

The report went on to state that the application of sanctions and disinvestment would exacerbate an already serious situation. The Commission's findings were submitted to a plenary session of the Catholic Bishops in January 1987.   (15)

Chapter Eight
THE TRADE UNION DIMENSION

Calls for disinvestment and sanctions by various South African trade unions have always been highlighted by left-wingers in Western Europe and North America. That these statements, however, bear little resemblance to what most black workers feel, is becoming obvious. The contradiction of maintaining a facade of fighting for jobs and conditions, while publically and internationally demanding measures guaranteed to destroy the jobs of hundreds of thousands of black South Africans, is striking home.

The growth of the trade union movement in South Africa since the legalisation of trade unions in 1979 has been spectacular. As in Britain, however, the debate surrounding the exact role of unions has focused upon the cynical manipulation of trade unions and their members for overtly political ends. The South African labour market has been polarised by the emergence of unions more concerned for radical political agendas than with improving the economic conditions of workers. Because Britain has experienced numerous examples of politically-motivated industrial actions, it is not difficult to recognise a similar theme in South African industrial unrest.

The formation of the Confederation of South African Trade Unions (COSATU) in December 1985 was the culmination of four years of merger talks involving a number of unions. These included the Council of Unions of South Africa (CUSA), the Azanian Confederation of Trade Unions (AZACTU), Federation of South African Trade Unions (FOSATU) and the South African Allied Workers Union (SAAWU). The formation of a large federation of trade unions in South Africa has long been an objective of organisations such as the South African Communist Party and African National Congress as a step nearer to their goal of being able to unleash an all-encompassing general strike within South Africa. Not surprisingly, since its founding COSATU has consistently called for sanctions, its president Elijah Barayi stating that his organisation gave its "full support to disinvestment".(1)

COSATU's endorsement of sanctions, which could only adversely affect black workers in Southern Africa, has led to fierce criticism. Trade unions such as the Federation of Metal and Building Workers, the Clothing Workers Union and the newly formed United Workers Union of South Africa have all criticised COSATU's pro-sanctions stance. The Inkatha nationalist movement has also highlighted the Marxist-style centralism of COSATU:

"Some political movements in South Africa - instead of being membership-based - have now concentrated on literally poaching trade union membership through affiliation instead of building up their own powerbases.

The broad mass of black trade union members are rarely, if ever, consulted by these organisations before political decisions are made regarding vital issues affecting them - political affiliations and stances, sanctions and disinvestment are prime examples" (2)

Inkatha president Buthelezi has condemned COSATU outright for being a front for the pro-Soviet ANC terrorist organisation, accusing the union of seeking to use black workers to destabilise the South African economy. Chief Buthelezi has long been involved in securing worker and trade union rights in South Africa. As recognition for this commitment he received the George Meany International Human Rights Award from the giant American Federation of Labour-Congress of Industrial Organisations (AFL-CIO). He became the second holder of this trade union award - the other being Polish Nobel Peace Laureate, Lech Walesa, for his work with Solidarity.

The KwaZulu government supported the 1973 strikes by black workers in Natal and Chief Buthelezi has made his view on workers rights very clear:

"We accept the right to strike is the workers perogative. We will continue to stand behind all black workers if and when they feel that we should support them when they use their right to strike. We are prepared to do anything that is in the interests of workers" (3)

The contradictions of urging, through advocating disinvestment and sanctions, the destruction rather than promotion of job opportunities has caused considerable resentment from ordinary COSATU members. The large-scale job losses directly related to disinvestment have caused COSATU to backpedal on the issue. That pro-sanctions trade union leaders were on very thin ice could be seen from statements from leaders of the various affiliated COSATU components, and was not limited to COSATU-affiliates-as evidenced by Piroshaw Camay, general secretary of the large Black Consciousness-aligned 'Council of Unions of South Africa' speaking in early 1985:

"Apartheid is a crime against humanity and the majority of people are racially oppressed. Under these circumstances we would consider a call for total disinvestment, but we don't think this would work"(4)

This view was shared by Joe Foster, General Secretary of the Federation of South African Trade Unions (which subsequently dissolved with many of its members joining COSATU). Speaking in 1985, he outlined his then membership's view on punitive economic measures against South Africa:

"If I stand up in public and call for disinvestment, our members at Leyland would kill me" (5)

Criticism of COSATU's unpopular and unrepresentative sanctions stance has been so severe that COSATU vice-president, Chris Dlamini, appearing on the BBC 'Newsnight' programme in March 1987, denied that the union had ever called for disinvestment - although this in turn was later contradicted by COSATU general secretary, Jay Naidoo. Despite this obvious confusion, even among South African trade unionists, the overseas pro-sanctions propaganda machine keeps churning out its disinformation - as evidenced by publications of the British 'War on Want' campaigning group:

"Inside South Africa the largest federation of trade unions - COSATU - and the South African Council of Churches (SACC) have both called for disinvestment and other economic action against the apartheid government" (6)

Chris Dlamini's statement distancing himself from his previously stated beliefs attracted the immediate attention of Chief Mangosuthu Buthelezi:

"The very people who travelled the world campaigning for disinvestment and sanctions still have their jobs while the victims of disinvestment and sanctions are losing theirs in droves.

In the past week I have been amazed at the hypocritical manner in which vociferous proponents of disinvestment have been attempting to disassociate themselves from something which, clearly, is turning sour on them.

It is truly sickening to read the statements of people like Dr Allan Boesak and Mr Chris Dlamini who now appear to be trying to squirm out of their formers stances" (7)

Further contradictions surrounding COSATU's pro-sanctions stance were also highlighted by a recent report. Commissioned by COSATU, the Community Resource and Information Centre examined the economic effects of sanctions. Its conclusion, not surprisingly, was that sanctions could add a further two million to the ranks of the unemployed by the year 2000.(8)

Another example of the gap between pro-sanctions radical trade union leadership and their rank-and-file can be seen in the mining industry. Cyril Ramaphosa, high profile general secretary of the National Union of Mineworkers, has consistently called for sanctions. Both Ramaphosa and NUM president, James Motlasi, for example, visited Western Europe in mid-1986. Speaking at the British National Union of Mineworkers conference in July 1986, both called for sanctions. On their return the South African Chamber of Mines challenged the NUM to prove that the union's members approved of sanctions. While avoiding answering this challenge, the National Union of Mineworkers warned the Chamber of Mines in July 1986 of 'serious confrontation' if black miners were retrenched. Bearing in mind that retrenchment is an inevitable result of sanctions and disinvestment, the contradiction in Ramaphosa's stance is clear.

One prime example of leftist disinformation is the recent report "A Strategy for Sanctions Against South African Coal" by the 'Anti-Apartheid Movement' in the United Kingdom. In an attempt to legitimise the massive job losses inherent in this 'strategy' this report claims:

"Finally and above all sanctions against South African coal are an expression of international solidarity with the Black miners of South Africa, with their union, the NUM, with COSATU as well as with the wider anti-apartheid forces in South Africa as represented by the UDF and above all by the liberation movement of the oppressed people of South Africa, the African National Congress" (9)

What is becoming increasingly obvious is the variance between claims such as the above and the actual opinion of, in this example, the coal miners. A recent survey shows that two-thirds of black South African coal miners do not want sanctions. Commissioned by the German Africa Foundation in Bonn, the survey was carried out by the IMS Institute in Johannesburg and evaluated by the Emnid Institute in West Germany. GAF President Karl-Heinz Hornhues commissioned the survey in order to accurately assess black worker opinion in the light of claims by pro-sanctions lobbyists in Germany that blacks welcomed sanctions, even if they meant hardship and sacrifice. Mr Hornhues said the survey totally contradicted these claims.

"For those who regard sanctions as the 'magic cure' with which to end apartheid, the findings might give rise to a rethink...The argument that blacks accept sanctions and are prepared to bear the resulting sacrifices can no longer be advanced in this form" (10)

Despite this conclusive evidence that black South African coal miners reject punitive economic measures, the British National Union of Mineworkers, itself overwhelmingly based in the coal mining industry, is a leading advocate of sanctions - particularly against South African coal. The situation of white miners - themselves buttressed against any hardship resulting from unemployment, passionately demanding measures which would result in massive job losses among reluctant black coal miners - miners who do not enjoy social security or unemployment schemes - is one which has obvious contradictions.

The disinvestment from South Africa of the United States General Motors corporation provided a classic example of another contradiction of COSATU's stance on sanctions and disinvestment. The General Motors base in South Africa was in Port Elizabeth and its 3,500 black workers were represented by the COSATU-affiliate, the National Automobile and Allied Workers Union (NAAWU). Although both the COSATU and NAAWU unions support disinvestment, far from welcoming the move, the National Automobile and Allied Workers Union promptly went on strike complaining they hadn't been consulted, showing quite belated concern about jobs and conditions.

The actual outcome of the General Motors move was a particularly cushioned disinvestment with a South African consortium taking over the operation lock, stock and barrel. The new company is no longer bound to the liberal 'Sullivan' employment code, nor forbidden to sell its vehicles to the state.

No such cushion was provided when Eastman-Kodak totally disinvested in November 1986, putting 600 black workers out of jobs.

NOTES

CHAPTER 1

1   Dr D F Malan and Dr Hendrik Verwoerd were prime ministers of South Africa in the wake of the National Party's 1948 electoral victory, and were responsible for legislation entrenching apartheid as an integral part of South African society.
2   'Southern African Freedom Review', International Freedom Foundation, Vol 1 No 1 Winter 1987, p 20
3   'Southern African Editorial Services', No 83 May 1986
4   'Southern African Freedom Review', op cit

CHAPTER 2

1   Merle Lipton, 'Capitalism and Apartheid', London, 1985
2   'Disinvestment', Special Issue of *LEADERSHIP* magazine, Johannesburg June 1985
3   'International Herald Tribune', 4 June 1986
4   'Indicator South Africa', Summer 1987
5   'Disinvestment', op cit
6   Leon Louw, 'South Africa: The Solution', Amagi, Ciskei 1986
7   Clem Sunter, 'The World and South Africa in the 1990s', Johannesburg, 1987

CHAPTER 3

1   'Southern African Editorial Services', No 83 May 1986
2   Arnt Spandau, 'Southern Africa and the Western World', IEES, Reutlingen, 1984 p 24
3   ibid p 15
4   'British Trade with South Africa', UKSATA, London 1978
5   'British Trade with South Africa', UKSATA, London 1980 p 70
6   Cited in 'Star', 11 October 1985
7   'South Africa: The Business Approach', Confederation of British Industry, London, 1985
8   HANSARD, 28 June 1983
9   Channel Four News, 13 June 1986
10   Foreign Affairs Committee, House of Commons, 11 December 1985
11   HANSARD, 17 June 1986
12   'Business Day', 16 January 1987
13   ibid
14   'Southern Africa and the Western World', op cit
15   Cited in Johannesburg 'Sunday Times', 6 July 1986
16   ibid
17   Richard Moorsom, 'The Scope for Sanctions', Catholic Institute for International Relations, London 1986 p 23
18   'Southern African Editorial Services', No 86 May 1986
19   Arnt Spandau, op cit, p 29
20   'Sanctions', Defence and Diplomacy Study No 1, Washington DC 1987
21   ibid

22 'Southern African Editorial Services', No 85, 1986
23 'Financial Times', 13 October 1985
24 'South African Digest', May 8 1987
25 'Southern African Editorial Services', No 81, March 1986
26 'SADCC: Progress, Projects and Prospects', Economist Intelligence Unit, London 1984 p 67
27 SAES, No 81, March 1986
28 'Observer', 25 October 1987, p 14
29 'Southern African Facts Sheet', Bureau for Information, Pretoria, No 19, January 1987
30 'Southern Africa's Future: Europe's Role', Association of West European Parliamentarians for Action against Apartheid. The Hague Netherlands, 1987 p 4
31 'South Africa: Mainstay of Southern Africa', Department of Foreign Affairs, Pretoria, 1985 p 14
32 'Financial Times', 13 October 1985
33 ibid

CHAPTER 4

1   'Sanctions', Defence and Diplomacy Study No 1, Washington DC 1987
2   South African Press Association, 12 March 1987

3   Sixth Report of the Foreign Affairs Committee, House of Commons, Westminster Vol 1 HC 61-II
4   'Disinvestment', Special issue of Leadership magazine, Johannesburg June 1985
5   'INKATHA: The South African liberation movement', Inkatha, Ulundi, 1987, p 5
6   South African Broadcasting Corporation, 3 May 1986
7   Foreign Affairs Committee pp 97-8
8   ibid pp 72-3
9   ibid pp 204-5
10 ibid pp 205-6
11 'Cape Times', 28 June 1987
12 'The Testimony of Steve Biko', edited by Millard Arnold, Panther 1979
13 ibid
14 'Washington Times', 7 February 1985
15 'Pretoria Times', 10 September 1986
16 South African Press Association, 14 July 1986
17 Foreign Affairs Committee, pp 208-21
18 'Human Resource Management', Journal of the South African Society for Training and Development, July 1987
19 ibid
20 Supplement to 'African Business and Chamber of Commerce Review', Journal of NAFCOC, October 1985, p 3
21 'Post', Johannesburg, 27 April 1985
22 'Southern African Editorial Services', No 83, May 1985
23 'The Citizen', 10 October 1987

24   'South African Digest', 26 September 1986
25   'Argus', 20 March 1986
26   'Southern African Editorial Services', No 83, 1985

CHAPTER 5

1   Ann Seidman, 'The Roots of Crisis in Southern Africa', American Oxfam/Africa World Press, Trenton 1985
2   'South Africa Foundation News', Johannesburg, August 1986
3   'South African Digest', 30 October 1987
4   London 'Sunday Times', 3 August 1986
5   'Weekly Mail', October 16-22 1987
6   ibid
7   ibid
8   'SA Foundation News', op cit

CHAPTER 6

1   'Guardian Weekly', 4 August 1985
2   'International Herald Tribune', 4 June 1986
3   ibid
4   Foreign Affairs Committee II
5   'Disinvestment', Special issue of *Leadership* magazine, Johannesburg June 1985
6   ibid
7   ibid
8   ibid
9   ibid
10   ibid
11   'Daily Telegraph', Abridgement of the annual Anglo-American Corporation of South Africa statement, 11 July 1986 p 29

CHAPTER 7

1   Richard Moorsom, 'The Scope for Sanctions', Catholic Institute for International Relations, London, 1986
2   Foreign Affairs Committee 2, pp 208-21
3   ibid
4   ibid
5   'Steve Biko - I write what I like', edited by Aelred Stubbs, Heinemann, London, 1987 p 57
6   'Washington Times', 7 February 1987
7   'The Citizen', 10 October 1987
8   'Washington Times', op cit
9   'Africa Insight', Africa Institute, Pretoria, Vol 16 No 2, 1986 p 101
10   'Apartheid: How Much Longer?', Internationale Gesellschaft fur Menschenrechte, Frankfurt 1986
11   'Clarion Call', Inkatha, Ulundi No 3 July 1986
12   ibid
13   'Apartheid: How Much Longer?' op cit
14   'Why Sanctions?', War on Want, London 1987
15   'Business Day', 27 January 1987

CHAPTER 8

1   'Cape Times', 2 December 1985
2   'Inkatha: The South African liberation movement', Inkatha, Ulundi 1987
3   ibid
4   'Rand Daily Mail', 22 March 1985
5   ibid
6   Why Sanctions', War on Want, London 1987
7   'The Citizen', 12 March 1987
8   London 'Sunday Times', 21 June 1987
9   'A Strategy for Sanctions Against South African Coal', Anti-Apartheid Movement, London 1987
10 'Business Day', 28 September 1987

APPENDIX 1

SOUTH AFRICAN POLITICAL REFORM

1976
- South African sport desegregated

1977
- Racial clauses within the 1956 Labour Relations Act pertaining to job reservation legislation removed

1978
- Black South Africans granted leasehold home ownership rights

1979
- Black trade unions legalised
- Black trade unions given the right to strike and bargain collectively
- Racial clauses within the 1979 Unemployment Insurance Act removed
- Unemployment Insurance Board made multi-racial
- Afrikaans dropped as compulsory language in junior school education

1980
- Most hotels, restaurants, libraries and sports facilities made multi-racial
- State spending on black housing doubled

1981
- Racial wage discriminations prohibited
- Education made compulsory for black children
- Multi-racial President's Council begins debate on constitutional future
- Trade Unions desegregated
- Multi-racial Small Business Development Act introduced

1982
- Local government for black South Africans introduced
- Black South Africans join government and parastatal boards

1983
- New South African constitution introduced establishing a Tricameral Parliament with white, Coloured and Asian representation; and a multi-racial cabinet
- Local government elections for black South Africans
- South African universities desegregated
- Employment discrimination legislation scrapped

1984

- Coloured and Asians vote for their representatives in Parliament
- Educational parity for all grouping assured

1985

- Commitment to power sharing with black South Africans
- 75% of all whites in nation-wide poll would accept some form of power sharing with black South Africa
- Urban business districts made multi-racial
- 1950 and 1957 Immorality Act scrapped
- Prohibition of Mixed Marriages Act scrapped
- Multi-racial political parties allowed
- Clauses within the 1967 Environmental Planning Act, enforcing a ceiling on black workers on the Witwatersrand and in the Western Cape, repealed
- Forced removals ended
- Black South Africans granted freehold land ownership rights
- One citizenship for all South Africans promised
- A multi-racial cabinet appointed
- All racial clauses pertaining to immigration regulations within the 1972 Admission of Persons to the Republic Regulation Act repealed
- Nelson Mandela and other imprisoned ANC leaders offered amnesty if they renounced violence

1986

- National Statutory Council created to develop a new constitution incorporating black South African political representation
- 1953 Reservation of Separate Amenities Act repealed
- 1964 Black Labour Act 67, used in part to enforce influx control, scrapped
- 1945 Blacks (Urban Areas) Consolidation Act 25, repealed, ending all influx control of black movement into urban areas
- 1971 Black Affairs Administration Act repealed
- South African citizenship restored to homeland blacks
- All-white Provincial councils abolished
- Multi-racial Regional Services Councils established

APPENDIX 2

POLITICAL ORGANISATIONS IN SOUTH AFRICA

AFRICAN NATIONAL CONGRESS: Formed originally as a liberal black nationalist organisation in 1912, but drifted increasingly into the orbit, and subsequent control, of the South African Communist Party leading to its banning in 1960. Currently sponsored by the Soviet Union, it is a Marxist terrorist organisation with strong links with the PLO.

AFRIKANER WEERSTANDSBEWEGING: A paramilitary national-socialist organisation formed in 1974.

AZANIAN PEOPLE'S ORGANISATION: A black consciousness movement formed in 1978. AZAPO seeks a unitary, socialist state in South Africa. Exclusively black in membership to the point of racism.

BLACK PEOPLE'S CONVENTION: A black consciousness-orientated group formed in 1972, excluding any white membership. Banned in 1977.

CONSERVATIVE PARTY: Formed in 1982, by extreme right-wing Members of Parliament expelled from the National Party, it is now the Official Opposition in the South African Parliament. In the May 1987 general election it gained the support of 27% of the white electorate.

HERSTIGTE NASIONALE PARTY (Reformed National Party): A white supremacist Afrikaner party formed in October 1969 by disgruntled National Party MPs and members. Demands a return to strict apartheid and immigration controls.

INKATHA: Formed in 1975, it is a predominantly Zulu-orientated political organisation based in Natal, with branches in the Cape, Transvaal and Orange Free State. It is the largest political organisation in South Africa with a membership of 1.3 million.

LABOUR PARTY: The main Coloured political party in South Africa, advocating a democratic, multi-racial society.

NATIONAL PARTY: The ruling party in South Africa.

NATIONAL PEOPLE'S PARTY: The ruling Indian party in the South African Parliament.

NEW REPUBLIC PARTY: Formed in 1977 by former United Party members seeking a multi-racial, federal government based on power-sharing.

PAN AFRICANIST CONGRESS: Formed originally in 1959 as a breakaway party from the ANC - in protest at white SACP influence - and banned in 1960, the PAC is now a Sino-orientated Marxist movement.

PROGRESSIVE FEDERAL PARTY: Created in 1977 from a merger of a United Party faction with the Progressive Reform Party, it was the official opposition from November 1977 until May 1987. The party seeks multi-racial power-sharing within a federal constitution, and the abolition of all discriminatory legislation.

SOUTH AFRICAN COMMUNIST PARTY: Formed in 1921, the SACP is one of the oldest communist parties in the world and has a reputation as the most loyal to the Soviet Union. In alliance with the ANC.

UNITED DEMOCRATIC FRONT: Created in 1983 as an umbrella grouping for socialist and Marxist-orientated organisations within South Africa. It has played a key role in the ANC/SACP's strategy of "mass mobilisation" to render South Africa ungovernable. Many of its affiliates have been responsible for black on black violence.

KING ALFRED'S COLLEGE

LIBRARY